Teach Better, Save Time, and Have More Fun: A Guide to Teaching and Mentoring in Science

Penny J. Beuning
Dave Z. Besson
Scott A. Snyder

With an Annotated Bibliography by Ingrid DeVries Salgado

Published by Research Corporation
for Science Advancement

Design by Godat Design

ISBN 0-9633504-9-7

RESEARCH CORPORATION
for SCIENCE ADVANCEMENT
A foundation dedicated to science since 1912.

4703 East Camp Lowell Drive, Suite 201
Tucson Arizona 85712

Contents

Foreword

As faculty members at research universities, we decided to pursue this career because we enjoy the challenges of teaching, research, and integrating these activities. However, we realize in the early stages of one's faculty career, massive amounts of precious time can be lost to "reinventing the wheel," particularly when it comes to teaching and mentoring. Research on early career faculty shows that many spend far too much time preparing for class and on other teaching duties, often at the expense of their scholarly work and research portfolios (Boice, 2000). New faculty in the physical sciences often face additional and unique challenges from the rigors of large lecture classes, often composed of diverse student populations with differing levels of interest and capabilities. Furthermore, faculty are often required to integrate parallel laboratory courses into their large lecture syllabi, labs which ideally are well-integrated with lectures to create an educational whole and that require the marshalling of diverse resources for success.

The Cottrell Scholar Award recognizes faculty at research universities for their dedication and excellence in both teaching and research. We surveyed 241 Cottrell Scholars in 2012 — 2013 asking them about practices that they have found to be effective in enhancing student learning and their own enjoyment of teaching. We asked them to think back to their earliest teaching experiences as faculty members and to reflect on what they might have done differently, as well as to think about what advice they wished they had received when they started their careers.

From the 46 faculty who responded to our survey, approximately 50% reported that they were given no advice or mentoring before teaching their first class; hence this text. We hope that it may find use as a personal handbook, directed primarily towards junior faculty, but with sufficient generality to find relevance with tenured faculty as well. In contrast to many (very useful!) quantitative measures of "what works," this book is by design and by construction purposefully conversational and colloquial. Along with the text, which weaves together themes that emerged from the survey responses, we include some actual survey responses to personalize the content. In addition, some other faculty who are not necessarily Cottrell Scholars contributed to the content independent of the survey. Information and ideas were also obtained at the annual Cottrell Scholars conference, attended by past scholars as well as science education experts and leading policy and government officials. It should be pointed out that those named here do not necessarily endorse the entire content in this book; the main text, its organization, and commentary is principally that of the authors. At the end, you will find a resource list and a bibliography that provides brief summaries of some of the resources in the literature which we and others have found useful should you wish to delve further into a particular area.

Acknowledgments

First and foremost, we would like to acknowledge Research Corporation for Science Advancement, which provided the funding for this project. In particular, we thank Silvia Ronco and Kathleen Parson for moral and technical support. Not only did they provide direct assistance to our efforts, but the environment and discussions which they provided and fostered at the Cottrell Scholars conferences tremendously aided and furthered our goals.

Second, we owe a deep debt of gratitude to those Scholars who answered the survey and who provided feedback on the book. We asked you to think back to some of your earliest experiences in teaching and leading research projects and how your philosophies have changed over time, and your responses have profoundly shaped this text. We are also very appreciative of Arthur Winter for the idea of "Facts that were Problems." Of note, some Cottrell Scholars provided feedback on the project as a whole: Martin Gruebele, Mike Hildreth, Geoff Hutchinson, Mike Moldwin, Jenny Ross, and Brad Smith. We sincerely thank several outside reviewers who took the time to give us feedback on drafts of this book and contributed many valuable suggestions for improvement: Colleen Byron, Moses Chan, Erin Cram, Vicente A. Talanquer, Jodi Wesemann, and Victoria L. Williams. We also wish to thank those who contributed to and/or reviewed this book but preferred not to be publicly acknowledged.

Finally, our research groups and families deserve our sincere appreciation for their support of our science, our efforts in teaching, and our careers in general.

Preface/Introduction

"When I taught University Physics I (calculus-based mechanics) for the first time, it was miserable. Although it was the first time that I used 'peer-instruction' clickers as a standard part of my lectures, and expected that to directly translate into an improved in-class experience, very early on I realized my prospects for the semester were poor. There were a couple of individuals in the class who consistently emailed me with (sometimes virulent) complaints about the level of work in the class, and I slowly began to withdraw from the class as a whole. As time went on, I found myself increasingly adopting a bunker-mentality as the time I was devoting to rear-guard actions began to cut into my research time. Somewhat predictably, my teaching evaluations were as bad as I had ever received as an instructor, and were complemented by my realization that very little learning had been achieved, either. From where I was, anything had to be an improvement.

The following spring I approached things somewhat differently. I hired an undergraduate teaching assistant to handle all my direct e-mail and began a practice of concertedly interacting with the class, on both an individual as well as a collective level, after the assignment of each clicker question. By circulating through the class after assigning a question, I not only got first-hand information on what problems students were having, but also built, to a small degree, personal relationships with some of the students (certainly it helped me learn their names). This was helped considerably, by having the lab TAs present during the lectures, as well - they not only had an opportunity for additional interaction with the students, but also were more aware of what was happening in lecture and how best to synch that with the laboratory component of the course

Not surprisingly, my evaluations that semester were somewhat better over the previous year. Although I didn't evaluate it numerically, my impression is that the overall learning experience also improved. Certainly, the class performance on exams, which I regarded as comparable (or greater) in difficulty than exams I had given in previous semesters, was markedly better. The obvious question is how much of this improvement was the result of steps taken to make the clicker questions more effective, and how much was simply improving the overall class environment, on both sides of the lectern. I believe it's actually mostly the latter, although certainly a more interested clientele is also a clientele most likely to approach the course material positively."
Dave Besson

"Probably my most successful teaching experience was a complete re-vamp of the Introductory Physics sequence targeted at the Engineering students. The sequence was reduced from a three-semester version to two semesters. To keep the credit hours high, a mandatory recitation section was added. I got to pilot the sole section of this course, basically creating the whole course structure from scratch. I switched my lectures over to a "Think-Pair-Share" style, and created group problem-solving exercises for the recitation sections. I learned a lot that semester and made more than a few mistakes, since it was only my second semester teaching. It was extremely valuable, however, when the course was put in "production" mode the following semester, with three instructors and almost 500 students. The second time through, things ran much more smoothly, and my lectures were a lot more "seamless." This curriculum change led to several new initiatives around campus.

For the first time, we initiated a teaching training program specific to physics instruction for all our incoming physics graduate students. This was mostly to put all of the students who run the discussion sections at a higher level of preparedness, but we also included lab instruction, grading strategies, etc. The training is now part of the standard graduate student orientation. The training session usually consists of an introduction given by a member of our campus Learning Center on the importance of good teaching and including some tips for student-TA interaction and time management. We then will have the TAs go through a group learning exercise with one of the faculty playing the role of the exercise facilitator, so that they can see different aspects of how to run a group problem-solving session. We also will typically include a brief lab exercise so that they can get a feel for what the labs will be like, and how we might conduct them. This has resulted in a TA corps that is much better prepared for the sorts of things we are asking them to do.

As an added bonus, other departments have adopted the group-problem-solving paradigm for their recitation sections instead of having them be some place where a TA merely solves homework problems. The experiences with that course, and the success that it had, largely established my teaching credentials both within the Department and around the University."
Mike Hildreth

Part I:
Developing and Delivering Effective Courses

1

Starting and Staying Strong

Many experienced teachers recommend that you sit in on courses of effective teachers, keeping in mind that such individuals may not necessarily be those with the best student evaluations at the end of the semester. Your department chair or mentor can usually recommend an instructor or two who would be most appropriate. It is especially useful if the course is at a similar level as yours or even a different section of the same course. Note what the instructor does that seems effective to you. How does the instructor interact with students? How are concepts explained and questions handled? Are relevant examples given? How does the instructor convey enthusiasm? What are the students doing? Are they paying attention or surfing the web on their phones waiting for the class to end? How do students interact with each other, if at all? What preparation is expected of students prior to class, and how are they held to account for that preparation? After sitting in on a few classes, it can be helpful to meet to discuss how the instructor views his or her teaching practices and their effectiveness. Similarly, ask to borrow materials from others, including sample syllabi, lecture notes, demonstration notes, and exams. Then adapt these to your own style and your students' needs and interests.

Setting the Tone

A good, positive first day of class sets the tone for the rest of the term. Setting yourself up for this great start to the new term requires some advance planning. Prepare as much as possible before the first day of class so that you can present a coherent, organized plan for the semester. Along these lines, very early in the term establish your own infrastructure for taking notes about what worked and what you would change as the semester progresses. This can be a note in your binder of class notes, a document on your computer, or even the syllabus file so that when you open this document to revise it for the next term your notes will be obvious.

One highly recommended strategy is to identify your learning goals for the course and plan the entire course around those goals. Such a "backwards-design" strategy centered on learning goals not only will help you prioritize material, but also will maintain your focus throughout the semester as you decide what you should teach and make the core of your course. Rather than planning a class chronologically, you should consider what you want your students to know or understand and to be able to do at the end of your course and then plan the course material and assignments around those goals. In that vein, it may make sense to consider critical elements and learning outcomes/goals for specific units or topics of the course, especially the first time teaching a course, to break down that larger task into more manageable chunks. This global analysis may also help you decide what types of teaching strategies you will employ. For example, if you want your students to learn and/or improve their critical thinking skills, a critique of a published paper or an analytical essay may be a more useful assignment than a quiz. If your students do not have many opportunities to practice their communication skills, a paper and a presentation or a presentation of a laboratory report may make more sense than a written exam. Your learning goals may also lead you to assign group work or use a specific active learning strategy. Deep learning of concepts and eliminating misconceptions about material and how students can best engage and master it requires repetition. Therefore, using your learning goals to structure the term can naturally lead to that form of repetition necessary for learning, which includes, for example, exposure to concepts from multiple perspectives and working many problems with slight variations. Moreover, identifying these goals in advance will make your life much easier and will allow you to present your comprehensive strategy to your students.

> "When I taught general chemistry a second time, I decided to come up with a list of five different concepts that I wanted the students to really understand and to hopefully retain several years after completion of the course. Some of these concepts included: collision theory of reactions, the meaning of an equilibrium, the concept of pH, chemical bonding in molecules, and mass-energy equivalence. My approach now is to underline these fundamental principles as we go through the course. I develop and reinforce these concepts through the duration of the semester and try to test conceptual understanding on exams."
> **Anonymous**

When you present your syllabus on the first day, ask for feedback from your students. You can set the expectation for active engagement by having students discuss some aspect of the syllabus in pairs or small groups, such as identifying core aspects of the course or how prerequisites specifically helped them prepare for your course; you can then have them report to the class. Moreover, write your syllabus to allow yourself flexibility. For instance, you can indicate that the dates of specific topics or exams are tentative or include a disclaimer to that effect. You might also consider allowing students to set their own grading criteria or schemes within certain ranges for specific assignments. The following, however, are critical:

- Set high (i.e. "tough") expectations at the beginning of the semester and resist the temptation to be too casual, especially if you appear younger than you are or are female. You can be more forgiving later, which will be much appreciated. However, do not be rigid or punitive just for the sake of it; students can face unexpected challenges that hinder their goals as well, and openness to their concerns can be extremely valuable in building esprit de corps and belief in your course and you in general terms.
- Write a defensive syllabus, meaning that you set clear expectations for respectful behavior and student etiquette in general (including email use, policies on late work, cheating, exam rescheduling, etc.).
- Be explicit about your expectations for the use of any type of electronics (allowed, forbidden, or allowed under certain circumstances).
- You may want to state that you expect all students to complete course evaluations, especially if low response rates are typical at your institution.
- Write a detailed syllabus and try to stick with the schedule as much as possible. Include deadlines and exam dates (even if tentative). Many college students find their newfound freedom a challenge and providing structure in your class will help them.
- Do more than go over your syllabus on the first day of class. Dive in to content, provide specific examples of what students will learn (an appetizer if you will), or do a review of important concepts with which you expect the students to be proficient. Incorporate active learning at this point; for example, students could work in pairs or small groups to review important background knowledge that they should have and then report back to the class. See below for tips on how to best manage such experiences.

When a student requests policy exceptions in the rush of the beginning or end of class, it can be very helpful to your own organization and overall management of the class to stall by saying: "Let me get back to you." Then, consider the implications, make a decision, and let the student know. It can be hard to make a good decision under these "quick-fire, cold-call" conditions, so it is certainly reasonable to delay for a bit. You may also want to keep a note of what you did to make sure you handle requests consistently as well as for future reference, as students will talk to each other about different components of the course.

Be transparent; explain to students why you teach a certain way and why you have specific expectations. For example, "Research (or, in the absence of hard data, "My own experience") has shown that students who come to class regularly perform better and earn higher grades. I would like ALL of you to earn good grades in this class, so I will require regular attendance." Similar discussions with your TAs will not only help ensure consistency in the course, but also contribute to the professional development of the TAs. Justify your grading criteria. Let students in on your strategy and how you view assessment.

> "Although I was not given any advice myself, I have some advice to new faculty.
> 1. Communicate to your students. Treat them like adults and explain how you are teaching them and why. Justify the grading structure of the course.
> 2. Give the students the ability to earn back missed exam points by redoing the exam problems. They get a second chance to learn, and they think you are nice.
> 3. Be a "hard-ass" at first and become nice later, or else they will walk all over you. I think this is especially important for female instructors, but it is a good practice for anyone.
> 4. Treat the syllabus as a contract with the students. Communicate it to them well. Include all the information needed for the entire course. Give them the opportunity to make changes on the first day. They never have any changes to make, but they appreciate being asked. See the paper from Cottrell Scholar Sarah Keller [J. Chemical Education, which is included in the Bibliography] on writing a good syllabus. I used this article when I first started, and it was invaluable."
> **Jenny Ross**

> "I allow students to compose their own grading scheme for a third-year Thermal Physics course within ranges I specify for each aspect, such as problem sets, midterms, final, independent project. In all but one case, the students performed better with their own grading scheme than with the default scheme of the course. This idea came from a similar style of evaluation used by my [former professor] though he allowed students to weight the final exam as little as 0%, which I did not permit."
> **Nancy Forde**

One way to set expectations is to directly tell students how much time outside of class you expect them to spend on this class; a typical equivalence is three hours of out-of-class time per one credit hour of in-class time, but even more time might be necessary and it may not be even throughout the semester or quarter. And, of equal importance, what will they be doing during this time? You can discuss with students some study strategies that you have personally found useful, such as re-writing class notes after class to help reinforce material as well as to identify areas of confusion, working extra practice problems, meeting in a study group to work through problems and discuss material that is unclear, attending office hours, and reading the text and taking notes, rather than highlighting. Drawing diagrams and concept maps can certainly be useful for organizing ideas (more on this below). Reviewing content and going over exams is also helpful for solidifying understanding. Intriguingly, science students often do not feel that they need to come prepared to class, especially if they are being lectured at for the entire class time (i.e. passive learning). Consider, for example, that most of them in their English discussion course would certainly have read the book ahead of time; suggest that the same is critical for your course, whether it is predominantly lecture or not.

It is helpful if students think about the material before class. You can ensure this by giving pre-class quizzes, homework, or short writing assignments online, or a brief quiz at the beginning of class. Or, alternatively, give other pre-lecture activities online, such as a short video, demonstration, or reading assignment. Students generally appreciate quizzes or practice questions before an exam to help them assess their preparation for that assessment and to help them focus their studying. Even in a laboratory class, mini-lectures and demonstration videos can be provided in advance so that class time can be dedicated to more detailed issues like data analysis and interpretation.

"One misconception I had comes from the students themselves. I often teach the first semester of introductory physics. Students, especially those coming straight from high school, often have the idea that someone should "teach" them physics. I try to disabuse them of this notion the first day of class, by telling them that I am there to help them *learn* physics, but teaching them physics is not something I can do. Learning is an active partnership between instructor and student. Many of them don't understand that the process of grappling with concepts and figuring out how to apply them requires actual *work* on their part. Each student has to understand for themselves how they learn, and this can be a difficult process. Often, students who didn't have to work hard in high school don't know how they learn best, and it comes as a shock to them when they realize that they really didn't understand a concept or a technique as well as they needed to. They have to figure out how to approach the concepts, and which techniques or ways of visualizing the concepts work best for them. Each person is different in that respect, and the only way they can discern what is best for them is to work at it by doing problems or other exercises, forcing themselves to think their way through the concepts. It's hard to say what is the best way to prepare students for the work that they will need to do, since many of them think "Oh, I'm fine — that's not my problem" as they start the semester. I was one of those students, and it took me years to figure out what I need to do in order to absorb new concepts. Having sympathy, being encouraging, and pointing out different ways that the students can prepare themselves and self-test their knowledge are probably the most important things one can do to help the students along this path."

Mike Hildreth

"Communication. Just reminding the students that you are there to teach them and that these methods are the best way for them to learn. Remind them that no matter how stern, entertaining, or smart you are, the actual learning can only be done by them - it is in their hands. Remind them that they will learn best when they apply themselves. Communicate the grading rubric and stick to the "contract" of the syllabus."

Jenny Ross

Help students understand what they will learn and gain in skills in addition to the specific course content. These items can be listed as learning goals or outcomes of the course on the syllabus and should be highlighted when you discuss your syllabus in class. For example, most science classes will teach analytical reasoning and problem-solving skills. A more specific analysis of your course could indicate that students will learn how to make decisions with limited information or be able to analyze problems to determine the most useful information for solving them, in which case they are learning to disregard extraneous information. Students are likely to improve communication skills in classes in which written reports or medium- or long-form exam answers are expected and you give them feedback on writing or speaking. Group projects or even regular use of think-pair-share strategies will also improve communication skills as well as their ability to work in teams and support each other in their shared educational journey.

Critically, do not assume that your students will have strong backgrounds or know and/or remember material from courses that are prerequisites for yours. It can be instructive to give students a short, well-designed, ungraded quiz at the beginning of the term that covers information and skills that you expect them to have, so you can be aware of and address weaknesses effectively up front. The experience of taking the quiz can sometimes prompt students to use knowledge they might believe they have forgotten and can help students 'connect-the-dots' between concepts they did not previously fully appreciate were related. This strategy is more effective than simply asking students if they are familiar with something or know how to do something, as they may not realize exactly the type or depth of knowledge that you expect or may be unwilling to admit they do not know. Alternatively, you might discover that students already have some knowledge or skills and therefore you can go into more depth or use class time for something else

Obtaining Useful Feedback

Ask for feedback from students throughout the course, perhaps with a short online poll or notecards or clickers. This tactic will help you address problems before they become too large to be dealt with easily and will help you hone as well as amplify the strategies and activities that are working well for students more generally. Most of us do not look forward to receiving feedback, but often instructors learn from early- or mid-term evaluations that things are going fairly well, and that can be a springboard for future successes. You can also discuss the results of a mid-term evaluation with your class and explain to them how you are making adjustments in response to the feedback you received. Students are generally quite appreciative that you took their concerns seriously. They also appreciate that you are giving thought to the way you teach and trying to maximize their outcomes as well; some faculty, unfortunately, do not take as much care.

There are a number of ways that you can obtain useful feedback. A written or electronic mid-term evaluation is useful and relatively fast. Some course management programs allow you to take a poll, although you will probably want to be sure that you can maintain each student's anonymity. Peer evaluation is often useful; you could ask colleagues from your own, or another, department to sit in on a typical class and provide their impressions. Staff from a campus teaching and learning center or education department may also be available to provide feedback in this way. Many people find it helpful (though also sometimes painful) to have a lecture recorded, which they can watch privately and assess their own teaching. You could appoint a student focus group or student representatives of the class to give you feedback on student perceptions of the class. To avoid accusations of favoritism, you could alternatively ask TAs to fulfill this role, as well as have your TAs try to provide you any "word of mouth" information that they have heard or picked up on during their recitation or laboratory sections. Feedback that is more focused specifically on student learning is discussed below in the section on Formative Assessments.

> "I was thrilled that my class would eagerly engage in discussions during and after clicker questions. I wanted to let people continue their discussions quietly, even after I picked up the lecture again, because it helped make the room feel more energetic in my late-afternoon class. However, several students pointed out in their mid-term evaluations that this was distracting and made it difficult to pay attention. In the next class, when the chatter continued, I asked those students first if they had any remaining questions, and when they said they didn't, I asked them to please stop talking because it was distracting. One of them looked quite offended, so I explained that this was feedback I had obtained in the mid-term evaluation, and if there were questions or more discussion was needed, they should speak up and we would continue the discussion, but if not, the chatter should stop because it made it hard for others to pay attention and learn. Everyone seemed satisfied with this explanation and in fact for the rest of the semester I rarely had to remind students to re-engage with the class at large after discussions."
> **Penny Beuning**

Conveying Enthusiasm

First and foremost, the most effective teachers convey enthusiasm for their subjects and courses and conduct courses in an engaging and professional manner. No amount of electronic gimmickry can compensate for a listless and soporific presentation. One simple way to meaningfully convey enthusiasm and engage students is to introduce relevant examples from the real world and/or recent news and popular culture. Put the material in context for students, both in the context of the world around them and in the context of the other courses they have taken or may take in the future. Utilize a variety of examples to help students from a wide range of backgrounds and learning styles. Making course content relevant to the future professions of students can also be motivating. This goal is the most straightforward in tailored courses (e.g., Physics for Engineering, Chemistry for Health Sciences), but can also be done in courses with diverse student backgrounds and education goals, by, for example, surveying the students at the beginning of class as to their planned careers. The science, technology, and health sections of major newspapers or news outlets are wonderful sources of material for this purpose. Major regulatory issues facing the United States or the world at large are also good sources, as are the news sections of major scientific journals. One way to increase relevance and immediacy is to assign students to bring in relevant news stories and explain how they relate to the course. This removes some of the burden on you as the instructor, engages students, and gives students a way to earn points other than in exams, which they generally welcome. Most students leave their science courses with little or no appreciation for the relatedness of different areas of science or even different courses in the same field. If you make the connections explicit, that problem can be solved!

One additional way of expressing your own enthusiasm for teaching the subject and of engaging students is experimenting with different pedagogical techniques. Getting students to interact with each other during lecture, for example, by using group projects or group discussions or debates, can build a sense of community in your classes. Consider making your problem sets and office hours group sessions as well (discussed in more detail later). Use a variety of presentation media and styles, for example, question-and-answer, lecture, videos, demonstrations, think-pair-share, peer discussions, etc. Not only does this add variety to class time and other times of student interaction, it usually signals to students that you have put effort into effective use of their time. These approaches will also help to ensure that you have fun with your classes.

Motivating Students to Learn

At the most basic level, the majority of students are principally motivated by earning good grades. However, in more general terms, students will learn and retain much more if they are motivated by other factors, such as a desire to learn, a belief that they can succeed, and a belief that you care about their success as well. This helps explain why classes that are "curved" up to ensure a large fraction of high grades do not always have high student satisfaction; although the curve can ameliorate grade anxiety, it often still leaves the student feeling disconnected from the course material, and even unsatisfied with how readily their goal of a good mark may have been attained. Remind those students who are struggling that this is part of the learning process, ensure them that they are making progress, and give some positive feedback. Convey your belief that students can be successful in your course. One simple tactic, even applicable in larger courses, is to email a student after an exam and indicate to them how happy you were that their mark had improved from their previous performance; in short, act like an effective coach, and your student-athletes will respond!

"How do you motivate students to learn? Many little things that don't slap it in their faces:
- Announcing that computer homework and book homework will be featured verbatim on exams, so do it all to be prepared.
- Spending a significant fraction of the time, at least one-third of the class time, in the classroom engaging students with questions, demonstrations, and concepts — not just the facts.
- Being available for office hours and one-on-one mentoring, even though it is very time consuming.
- Little surprises like an impromptu tour of your lab for students coming to office hours.
- Giving some complex problems that require multiple skills they have learned to be put together.
- Having a narrative in the course, like a good play. This is totally missing from current generation textbooks."

Anonymous

"I've never found a substitute for a face-to-face conversation with a student to help that person understand the material, feel more motivated (or less discouraged), and participate more in their own learning. I never get to speak with all of my general chemistry students, as hard as I may try. Last year, I was inspired by the digital warning notices that our Dean asks us to do for at-risk students. After each exam, I sent e-mail messages to students who were (1) consistently doing well, (2) experienced major improvement, or (3) dramatically dropped in score as compared to a prior exam. After that, I interacted more with the best performing students and others sought help. After the third exam, I emailed the students who represented the average and had little variance to applaud their consistency and acknowledge their efforts. This took some time, but I know I am an underutilized resource. While I can keep myself busy, there was enough time to send out these messages. The result was the positive effects of a small amount of personal interaction that we don't usually have in the large classes."

Rory Waterman

"One year our department offered an honors section of intro chemistry for the first time, and I volunteered to teach it. For the most part, the course was a dream — I loved the cohort of students as they were by-and-large intelligent and self-motivated. Attendance was high and I generally had great buy-in from my students in terms of doing the assigned work and studying (and performing well) on the increasingly difficult tests. However, I had a few students who were becoming increasingly exasperated with their poor performance. They were clearly trying as hard as they could, but were spinning their wheels — the material was just not sticking and they were on trajectories for Ds (or worse) in the course. It was past the drop date, and a couple of them were even trying to see if there was a way that the dean could make an exception as they were afraid for their grades. Instead of encouraging them to drop, I decided to get the students together and form a 'support group' just for them. We met at least once a week for a few hours, and worked on problem after problem so that I could catch their mistakes, and so that they could see where they were going wrong in each type of problem in a supportive atmosphere. The three students became increasingly confident (not just in our sessions but in asking questions in the lecture as well) and I could feel things improving. Indeed, they improved markedly in the last hourly exam and the final. You can't imagine how happy and relieved they were to earn two Bs and an A(!) in the course, and I was very proud of how they worked to transform their understanding of the material."

Boyd Goodson

Your students are most likely not like you, but then again, you may not have been who you remember. As much as possible, state your assumptions and what seems obvious to you. As an expert, you have a lot of specialized knowledge at your disposal and it may be difficult to remember what it was like to learn this material for the first time. Consider looking back at your own class notes from when you took a course to remind yourself of what you learned for the first time at a similar level. Stating your assumptions will help students feel that the class is more within their control and helps establish a culture of fairness.

Draw connections between what students already (should) know and what you want them to learn. Make connections to other courses, as well as to the larger picture of the field. Highlight connections among topics and concepts throughout your course. Using the "backwards-design" strategy outlined previously helps you stay focused on the overall picture and weave those themes throughout the course. Assess prior knowledge at the beginning of the term. Making such connections is especially important in introductory courses, whether at the undergraduate or graduate level, because they serve as a foundation for more advanced work.

Have a narrative for your course (and know what it is before the first day of classes!); absent an interesting story line, the course will suffer from a lack of continuity. Structure your course with coherent themes and goals and present material in an inquiry-driven way. For example, rather than present a fact, present the scientific approach, process, and questions being asked in the field, and the stories of the individuals who asked them and whose work led to the establishment of the concept. Explain how experimental outcomes are interpreted with models and how models are built and refined. Be explicit in helping students appreciate the intellectual framework of the course material.

For example, to convey the process of scientific discovery, you could incorporate modules of "Facts that were problems" in a class. These modules allow students to analyze data to (re-)discover the scientific facts that you want them to learn, and it will also help them develop critical and analytical thinking skills.

Some examples:

• Present the figures from Meselson and Stahl's paper (PNAS 1958, 44, 671) that showed that DNA replication is semi-conservative. Ask the students to come up with models of replication and to evaluate their models in light of the data presented in the paper that shows the distribution of isotopically-labeled DNA during replication.

• Have students use molecular models of the peptide backbone to derive a Ramachandran plot of allowed, or favorable, dihedral angles.

• Have students use balloons as electron pairs in order to determine bond angles of specific compounds.

> "In sophomore-level physics for majors at my university, the topics are a hodge-podge. I taught a course with Thermodynamics, Wave Mechanics, and Optics together, which are not so easy to make connections. In Thermodynamics, I had wanted to bring statistical mechanics into the concepts of the Laws of Thermodynamics and the concepts of Energy, Work, Heat, and Entropy. I alternated between macroscopic observations, driven by examples to lead group work and examples that students do, and microscopic first principles. We revisit each topic at both scales. Before the exam, I do a review in a class period where I go over all macroscopic thermodynamics together and all microscopic statistical mechanics together. Changing the order in the re-presentation before the exam allows the students to make new connections."
>
> **Jenny Ross**

Posing and Fielding In-Class Questions

One of the assumptions we often make when students do not have questions is that they actually understood what we taught them. There are many reasons why students may not have questions. Instead of asking, "Do you have any questions?" or "Any questions?" ask "What questions do you have?" and wait for a response. This approach conveys the message that you expect students to have questions.

Although you may have an unusually engaged class, many instructors have had the experience of asking a question and then facing the ensuing silence for what seems like an uncomfortable period of time. That response is normal, especially in a large lecture class where students may feel shy about speaking in front of so many others. Conventional advice is to wait at least 15-30 seconds before going on. You can also try restating and rewording the question. Sometimes restating the question exactly is helpful, as students get in the groove of taking notes and may not have expected your question or simply missed it. Then, reword the question to help students better understand what you are asking. One colleague provides a supply of lollipops that students can enjoy in class, to reduce the awkwardness of waiting for students to prepare to speak up.

Set the tone early, and get students talking at the start of the semester. Even in classes of 100 or more, students can be asked to introduce themselves or each other on the first day. Or you can take a poll on the syllabus or on their experiences in previous courses. Once the course is underway, there are other ways to elicit student comments and questions. Have the students discuss a topic, question, or problem in pairs and actively solicit questions during the discussion period. When you ask for questions and you are greeted with silence, have some prepared prompts, "In the past, students have been confused about..." or "When I first learned this, I wondered..." The latter method will also remind students that you were once a novice, too. If these are legitimate points of confusion, this will usually elicit nods and even additional questions. This approach may also be a way for you to identify misconceptions of students and then deal with them directly. And, when you do get questions, be sure to tell students that their questions are good ones. From the first time you teach a class, you can start keeping a list of points of confusion that you can use both to improve your explanations and as examples to prompt discussion. You can also use these points to frame debates by presenting several possible answers and asking students to determine the right one(s).

Listen to what students identify as their problems, both with course content and course mechanics. You can solicit this information online, through a course management site, or by using "one-minute" or "muddiest/least-clear point" short essays at the end of class. See section below on student assignments and assessments for more about such strategies.

A fun twist on the end-of-class short paper is to tell students that you will take any question or comment, which can include suggestions for improving the class, concepts that are unclear, or anything that the students are curious about. You can then decide how to answer, depending on the question. If something clearly needs more discussion in the next class session, plan to do that. The "curiosity" questions might prompt you to find some relevant information that provides real-world examples or adds depth to the class. Those questions that are far off-topic can be answered on a class website so that everyone in the class can read about it, but you do not necessarily need to use class time to address these topics. This task need not take much time. Even for off-topic questions, a relatively brief answer with a reference to further reading is probably enough.

> "It is important to find ways early on to engage the students. Since our classes at the undergraduate level are all General Education courses, we have the luxury that we don't have to worry that much about "getting through the material." Recognizing this wasn't immediately obvious to me and took some time. One of the more effective ways to engage the students is to give them points for turning in written questions at the end of class. I will discuss those questions as much as possible at the start of the following class. I will often expand on the question to show students why it was a good question or how it fit in with the material, even if the question may have been phrased poorly. I think it is important not to be condescending about any question that the students ask. I will postpone questions that concern topics to be covered later in the semester, and tell the students this. Of course, the class gets the first opportunity to give answers to these questions and this often leads to lively discussions."
> **Anonymous**

2

Class Preparation; Teaching a Course for the First Time

Quickfire question in class preparation: do you generally carry chalk or whiteboard markers in your regular bag? You might find it useful to have a dedicated teaching bag that has extra chalk, markers, AV cables, water, tissues or a cloth, etc. Alternately, you could set up a smaller bag to insert in your regular bag for teaching. If something about your classroom or the physical environment of your teaching is subpar, think creatively about how to fix it so that you are less distracted, or even request a different classroom. You could go so far as to have custom chalk holders made for holding the larger chalk used in large lecture halls, for example. If you use a computer, a remote slide-changer/pointer or even a remote tablet are invaluable for allowing you to roam around the room while still going through the course material. Keep in mind that even in the largest lecture halls, students can form groups of two or three with the people near them; you do not need a special classroom to have students work together.

Being an expert in the field, you might be tempted to think that you do not need to prepare very much and can lecture on the fly. In fact, that approach will rarely succeed, and astute students can tell when you are "winging it." Keeping your learning goals in mind is an important way to help you prepare your classes. Be as organized as possible in all aspects of the class. Prepare well for each class, especially when you are going to present examples, work through problems, or do demonstrations. In addition to preparing and organizing the material you will present, prepare the questions and problems you will pose to the students and how you will engage them in this work. Write down your planned active learning work; it will also be helpful to provide written instructions or tips for students as they engage in the activity. This strategy will be a time-saving one, because better, more detailed class notes will save you tremendous time the next time you teach the class.

While you are teaching the course, at the end of every class (or at least minimally at the midpoint of the term and the end of the term) write down what worked well and what you would do differently next time you teach this course. Note material that caused students to struggle. This will help you tremendously in improving the course the next time you teach it. If your course has a teaching assistant, negotiate stability — have the same student appointed the TA for the next time if possible. This is absolutely critical in gaining the efficiency of teaching the course the subsequent times.

Equally ideal, try to utilize teaching assistants from your research group, as you are likely to have a stronger relationship with them and their investment in your success could be higher as well. Critically, do not try to do everything at once; rather, keep refining your classes, using your notes and feedback from students and colleagues. This approach will help you continuously improve your classes as well as keep them fresh and keep you from getting bored.

> "When I first started teaching, I was under the impression that I could just "wing it" if I ran out of lecture material. I tried taking questions or suggestions for problems to work on the board from the students, without any advanced preparation. This was not a good idea. The first or second attempt at doing this ended in confusion when a student asked me to do a problem that was both subtle and not stated clearly in the text. After that embarrassing experience, I swore that I would always have way too much material for a given lecture, so that I would *never* come up short. It also pointed out in a rather painful way the importance of thinking through the presentation of complicated problem-solving steps well in advance. The things that might be obvious to me are often confusing for many of the students; shortcuts I might take are not necessarily the path that they would follow to a solution. I have found over the course of the years that providing the students with a clear and logical progression through the thought-process involved in solving a given problem, emphasizing general principles that can help them through similar problems, is one of the most effective things one can do to help them learn the concepts. That isn't to say that all flexibility is banished from my classes. I will often have students suggest their own ways of solving a problem I have presented, and following their train of thought, as long as I can see that it won't derail, gives them satisfaction that they have been able to see the solution to the problem using their own process. This is valuable reinforcement. It's possible to do this without a safety net, so to speak, because I have already worked the problem through to my own satisfaction and can be sure that the student's ideas will work."
>
> **Mike Hildreth**

Work through homework or problem sets that you are planning to assign in advance. Have a TA or one of your students check exams and proofread problems. This process helps you determine what you want to emphasize and ensures that your homework assignments will help students learn the things you would like them to learn; it will also make sure there are no mistakes or "impossible" problems that will deeply frustrate students. Then work through example problems in class and clearly explain the rationale for each step, possibly starting with an already-solved problem as an example. Present the logic of the problem. Work problems from multiple angles, explaining the logic and context of the problem. Use a range of examples, helping students see the generality of a fundamental concept and construct their own understanding. For example, if you are discussing the ideal gas law, examples could include the volume of a sealed plastic bottle on an airplane on the ground compared to in the air, tire pressure as function of temperature, a Mylar balloon, the bends, etc.

Begin each class by summarizing what was learned in the previous class. End each class by summarizing the material of the lesson and giving a preview of what is to come. This tactic requires some planning but should help students see the themes, narrative, and intellectual framework of the class. Such summaries can easily be done with active engagement of students. For example, you can pose a problem that requires students to apply what they learned already in the class or that combines several topics; the discussion can then be used to make connections explicit and to emphasize the main themes and narrative. Stating the main concepts of each class will also help students prioritize the material, which will lead to deeper understanding of important concepts. Some professors believe that students need to determine for themselves the most important material; however, this task is a difficult one for any student new to a field. Prioritizing material will help focus student efforts in studying and help them organize new material into the major themes you have highlighted — your job as an expert is to help provide that guidance.

Opinions differ on whether the instructor should hand out notes to the class or make them available on a course website as opposed to providing no notes. By providing notes, students can focus on your explanations rather than on trying to write their own notes. Giving prepared notes to the students can help you be more organized because the notes have to be prepared in advance and have to be clear enough to be useful. On the other hand, others believe that having notes available eliminates the incentive to come to class or to pay close attention to the instructor. One compromise is to provide minimally outlined notes that students complete during class, increasing the incentive to attend class sessions. In fields in which drawing diagrams is an important skill, for example organic chemistry and some areas of physics, the practice of drawing in class is critically important for development. Another alternative is to provide only oral recordings of your lectures, so students can listen to you speak again later with their written notes in front of them, providing them with additional opportunities to strengthen what was originally presented on their own time. See below under Technology for a discussion of using eLectures as an additional strategy.

Determine what services department staff can provide for teaching. You can ask them directly, or ask your chair or other faculty about the types of work staff can be expected to do for you or if they can give time to special projects. They may be able to order books for the bookstore and have lecture materials including the syllabus copied. They might also be available to type notes, prepare slides, or analyze course-related data, such as performance on specific exam questions by student. Whatever staff members do for you, remember to give plenty of advance notice for your requests and to thank them profusely for their help on your behalf.

Designing New Courses

Maybe you were hired with the expectation that you would fill a need by developing a new course. Perhaps this task is expected of all new faculty in your department or institution. In any case, developing a new course can be extremely time-consuming, especially if it also involves the accompanying laboratory section. First, do your homework, both by understanding what the expectations are for this course and by surveying existing, similar courses at your own and other institutions. Obtain syllabi, textbooks, and reading suggestions. Even redesigning an established course, say for example by integrating active learning such as clickers or peer instruction, takes a tremendous amount of time. Again, use existing resources and your network as much as possible.

If you are designing a new course, you should have assurances from the department that you will get to teach it several (ideally at least three) times. Each time you teach the course, adjustments can be made to correct what did not work well the last time. Do not worry too much about getting everything perfect the first time because that is impossible. Acknowledging that there will be mistakes that can be fixed in subsequent years makes the task less daunting.

It is the rare person who has the entire course fully prepared at the outset — whether a newly-designed course or even just a new preparation. Definitely have a detailed outline, with topics, readings, and homework, so you can give the students a roadmap for the entire term right at the beginning. Try to stay at least one or two complete lectures ahead of the class schedule so that you can anticipate problems and to provide the framework for the course.

Find out what is reasonable at your institution in terms of new course preparations. If you are well above the norm, you may want to have a serious chat with your mentors, department chair, and/or Dean about expectations for how teaching and course development are related to promotion and tenure and how best to use your time.

3

Utilizing New Pedagogy and Active Learning

"What students uncover is more important than what we cover."
Long-held teaching idiom

This section includes many recognized methods of teaching that increase student engagement, along with suggestions for effective implementation. Our suggestion, based on experience, is to start slow and not try to implement too many new ways of teaching at once. By implementing one or a few new practices per course, you will be able to gauge their effects on student learning and enthusiasm and will keep your courses fresh for you and the students. Implement changes to your course that you believe have a chance of being successful, as it will be difficult to convey enthusiasm if you are skeptical of your own teaching. The critical point is that strong evidence exists showing that active learning methods improve student outcomes by increasing engagement with course material and by providing more opportunities for assessment.

Don't Reinvent the Wheel
It is well worth your time to consult with others who have used methods you are interested in trying. Ask them what worked, what did not succeed, what they would change, and how students responded. Did they think it made the students more engaged? Did it help students learn more? How did they set the tone for the semester? How successfully were they able to engage students and do so consistently? It can be very useful to brainstorm with colleagues at other campuses as well, but keep in mind that your own campus may have specific resources for the types of things you want to try. For example, some institutions have centralized support for teaching with technology and you might not know about it unless you ask. Moreover, do not feel compelled to

adopt someone else's plan wholesale; rather, adapt it to your circumstances, your comfort, and your own strengths and attributes.

> "Getting the students to interact during lecture in small groups seems really important. The students value the chance to explain concepts and discuss with their peers, and I think it gives them confidence and also helps them sort out their own confusions. The learning should be active and continual during the lecture. I use Eric Mazur's Peer Instruction methods, using conceptual multiple-choice questions that focus the discussions."
> **Neepa Maitra**

A substantial number of survey respondents reported that they have adopted clickers or student response systems (65%) or non-electronic response systems (32%), think-pair-share strategies (38%), creative assignments such as student-produced videos (46%), or provided research experiences in teaching laboratories (43%). These practices were adopted primarily to improve student learning (95%) and to add variety to teaching the course overall (58%). These practices were reportedly received by students either very enthusiastically (41%) or positively (51%). No respondents reported negative receptions by students, although 7% report a "neutral" response from those under their tutelage. Although negative reactions by students were not reported in this particular survey, there is advice below about dealing with resistance of students and colleagues to innovations in teaching away from the standard lecture model.

> "Peer learning: Instead of doing examples for the students, I have the students do group work. This can be done with small groups of 2-4 students who are just sitting near each other. I have done this in small rooms and large stadium seating auditoriums, and it works great. I also like to walk around the room and pass by each group to make sure they are on track. Instead of office hours, try evening homework sessions. I have the students who are all working on the same problem get together in a group and work together. These will not only allow content coverage, but enable peer-learning that strengthens students' conceptual and problem-solving abilities. If another student already has the concept, they can educate each other. They are also time-saving (especially the homework sessions) because you can educate a small group instead of one student at a time. Further if another student already has the concept, they can educate each other. Very efficient."
> **Jenny Ross**

> "We use a quasi-POGIL [process oriented guided inquiry learning, in which teams of students work through designed course materials to discover and apply fundamental concepts] method. We utilize a number of guided activities in class. They allow the students to work on materials with breaks for answering questions and having mini-lectures. In some ways it has a POGIL style, but it is not a rigorous application of the POGIL methods by any means. We do not assign roles to the students. All the activities are not strictly inquiry. Students work through worksheets and periodically check-in to the class. For the "check-ins" we either have students share their answers on the document camera with the class, or simply answer out loud for the class with an explanation. Alternatively we have clicker questions for the whole class that we then have the students explain.

We also use readiness assessment quizzes [RAQ] to help students focus their study efforts and self-assess their knowledge before an exam. For the Readiness Assessment Quiz we again have students present their answers on the document camera and/or we have periodic clicker questions on the correct answer for each part of the RAQ.

I have attached a couple of examples of in-class work for clarification [in Appendix II]. The first is an activity that is used in a typical class. The second is a RAQ that is meant to help the students before an exam. All of these materials have been developed along with my colleague, Dr. Cynthia LaBrake, with whom I team teach."

David Vanden Bout

Fun, Innovative, and Active Learning

Have fun with your classes. Convey your love of the material by having fun with it. Make up songs or cheers to help students remember rules; for example, an entire class chanting "PV=nRT" at the tops of their voices is unlikely to forget the ideal gas law. Such devices can also serve as memory aids. If you doubt your creativity, there is plenty of material available from both books and websites, including poetry and songs about science (such as the Tom Lehrer element song!). Another option is to ask students for their own ideas or to have them come up with something in class. For common terms or concepts, you can give the students your own memory device/mnemonic and ask them if they know of others. For example, two common ways to remember electron flow in redox reactions are "LEO (loss of electrons is oxidation) the lion says GER (gain of electrons is reduction)" and "OIL (oxidation is loss) RIG (reduction is gain)." In organic chemistry, the phrase "Mary Eats Peanut Butter" helps students remember the first letters for methane, ethane, propane, and butane, the alkanes upon which many compounds are named based on having 1, 2, 3, and 4 carbons, respectively.

"When teaching Physics 102, our second-semester, first-year introductory Physics course for Life Science students, I decided to devise song lyrics to help students recall sign and direction conventions in E&M [electricity and magnetism]. I did this in the hopes that these would make it easy to recall the conventions, as there is no way to deduce them... In lecture, I show the videos first, because I have found that many of the students are not familiar with the songs. Also, I find that showing them some three-year-olds singing shamelessly lowers the barrier to their in-class participation. I manage to get all 200+ students on their feet and singing in lecture (though I fear if I brought out a video camera to record this, the majority would promptly sit back down!). I find that the one that they find most helpful is "Potential is Positive 'round a ... + charge." They will come to my office hours with questions about the potential at a given location in an arrangement of charges, and frequently, just saying, in rhythm "Potential is positive 'round a ..." will elicit a response of "plus charge," followed by "oh!" and an understanding of how to approach the problem."

Nancy Forde

Schemes and drawings are very useful learning tools, but they must be used with care. Students may not grasp the important features of a particular scheme, so it is important to explain each aspect and provide the conceptual background so that they can understand the depiction. Students can be asked to develop their own schemes or to provide the explanation for a given scheme to help them develop and deepen their understanding. Similarly, students may find analogies confusing or may miss the most important or relevant points of the analogy. Analogies should be explained or discussed in detail, emphasizing the most relevant and important points and where the analogy breaks down.

Use concept maps (you can often find examples in textbooks and in Figure 1, below) that you create or that students themselves devise to clarify the connections between concepts, facts, and fields. Concept maps help organize knowledge by showing connections between key terms, ideas, and information. Novice students may have trouble with this task, but by the later part of the semester, this exercise can help students see the connections between the concepts you have discussed. This approach is also an excellent way to get students to begin an "outline" for discussion sections of research papers.

A

Temperature	Mechanism	Catalytic Residues	NAMNAG
NAGNAGNAG	Lysozyme	Covalent intermediate	Mutations
Mass spectrometry	Structure	Binding Cleft	NAGNAG
X-ray crystallography	Function	Km	kcat
Substrates	Spectroscopic assay	Gln35	polysaccharides
Asp52	Glu35		

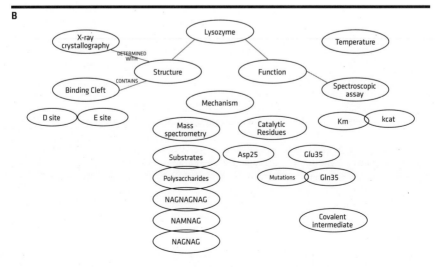

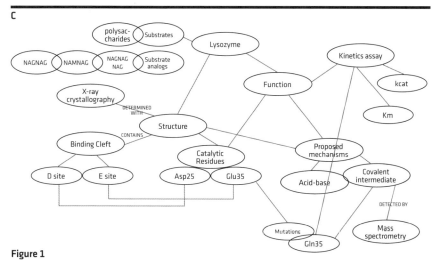

Figure 1

(A and B) Construct a concept map by listing relevant key words and concepts, then organize them in terms of their relationships. (C) Concept map for an article describing the mechanism of lysozyme. Examples courtesy of Linda Columbus.

Leading Discussions

Set ground rules and expectations for discussions. In the sciences especially, many students are not accustomed to participating in active discussions, so they may need coaching and direction to best understand how to participate effectively. You should also establish how credit will be given and the criteria for grading the discussion, such as preparedness, participation, and quality of interaction.

Teaching with case studies can be a particularly fun approach, as students can adopt the perspectives, and even the voices, of characters in a given situation. It can be difficult to understand all of the subtleties in one reading of a case in class, so have the students read it over more than once, or even better, give them the case in advance. You can also use several short cases which the students discuss in small groups and then have each group of students present their case, the issues it presents, and their proposed solutions to the class for further discussion.

> "Learning Activity: Debates in Class: To allow students more of an opportunity to voice their own thoughts in a course, and at the same time be exposed to a broader perspective on certain topics, I organize three debates during the semester on topics in a science course that lend themselves to debate. Examples include controversial viewpoints in US society on certain aspects of the course material, impacts of scientific discoveries on society, not yet fully established scientific theories, and the financial cost to society of doing the research. Depending on the length of the class period, 3 to 5 student volunteers are asked to serve as panel members. They

each prepare a statement on the particular debate topic that they read to the class during the debate. Each panelist's statement is followed by questions and discussion input from the audience (which consists of the other students). As a faculty member, I plan the flow of the debate by considering the topics the panelists have chosen to address, moderate the debate, and guide it in particular directions as students bring up relevant issues that deserve further discussion. I generally do not structure the debate ahead of time, that is, there is always enough discussion that I do not need to "create a controversy" by forcing the panelists to defend certain opposing viewpoints. A challenge that is somewhat difficult to overcome is that the level of preparation for the material can vary widely among panelists and audience, since this is in a general education science course, but I think most students get something out of the debates, and they are generally evaluated positively.

Participation credit is a part of the course grade and the debates are one component of obtaining this credit. The panelists gain such credit by volunteering to serve on the panel. The other students gain it by turning in written evidence at the end of each debate on their participation. This can include a brief summary of the questions they asked or other contributions they made during the debate."
Anonymous

Demonstrations

Demonstrations in class can convey enthusiasm and excitement for the material, and provide connections that are difficult to do through words alone. For low-cost and low-technology demonstrations, students can be shuffled around the room as atoms, stars, molecules, mirrors, or proteins, for example. You can even act out concepts with your body and/or props, enhancing the likelihood that the video students will take of you on their phones will go viral. Balloons can be used to illustrate atomic orbitals or concepts of gases and other fluids. Books or websites of science experiments for children can be good sources of simple, reasonably cheap, and safe demonstrations. These can generally also be adapted for laboratory experiments that students could do at home or in their dorms to reinforce topics, keep students engaged, or provide experiments for classes without a laboratory component. If you have no support staff, you may be able to negotiate for a small portion of TA time to assist in demonstrations or shared responsibilities among different instructors in a multi-section course.

Videos can be extremely useful for illustrating some concepts and can even substitute for demonstrations if demonstrations cannot be performed directly in class due to cost and/or safety concerns (such as the odors associated with the synthesis of Nylon, for example). There are simulations, illustrations, and videos of actual events available online as well as often being packaged with textbooks. When using demonstrations or videos in class, be sure to explain the context and how it relates to the course material. In other words, do not make a big boom or smoke cloud just because you can! Depending on how these tools are being used, you might ask students to make predictions of the outcome and/or to explain their observations. After the demonstration or video, discuss what the class saw, what it means, and how it relates to the course. For online videos, give the appropriate link, if available, so that students can view it again later on their own time. For demonstrations, it is sometimes possible to provide a written description or protocol so students can reproduce them on their own (for non-hazardous demonstrations) or a link to more information online. Demonstrations should be large enough to be seen by the entire class or small and safe enough to be passed around. Do not be afraid to do the demonstration or show the video more than once, even after some discussion, so that students can determine where to focus and what the important points are.

Finally, the Predict-Observe-Explain (POE) model helps to ensure that students actively engage with demonstrations. First, tell the students what you are going to do. Then, ask the students to predict what will happen; have them write down their predictions and the reasons for their predictions, then discuss them with the class. After a few reasonable predictions are made, carry out the demonstration, having students observe what happens. Then have the students describe their observations, provide an explanation, and discuss how the original explanations may need to be changed. This approach ensures intellectual engagement with the material that is presented in the demonstration, and is described in more detail in the Bibliography (Crouch 2004).

Integrating Lecture and Laboratory

Important concepts can be reinforced in the laboratory. Ideally, the laboratory exercises should be integrated with lecture topics, so that a given topic is covered in the laboratory at roughly the same time as in lecture. You may have little control over this component, particularly in large classes and in multi-section classes where you may have little interaction with the laboratory material. If you meet with the laboratory instructor or coordinator before the start of the term and obtain a copy of the lab materials as well as a schedule for the labs, you will then be prepared to discuss how the work done in the lab parallels and reinforces the material students are learning in lecture; bring your syllabus as well so that they can see your order of topic presentation. Be explicit about these connections. Inevitably, some labs get out of sync with lecture; keep this in mind and remember to give previews or reminders of the lab exercises that are related to your lectures at a given point. In addition, make sure that laboratory personnel are conveying the same message on topics as you are; nothing could be worse than having them "negatively" reinforce something you are trying to teach by contradicting your lessons and/or key points.

Discovery-Based Laboratories

The laboratory is the ultimate active learning experience. However, this opportunity can be squandered with lab exercises that involve following a recipe or set of instructions with little thinking involved. Some so-called "cookbook" labs may be necessary because, in addition to theory, students need to master the techniques of their field. Complementing them with labs in which no one knows the outcome in advance or, alternatively, the approach or analysis is not clearly specified, will allow students to apply their knowledge in solving an actual problem and confronting a scientific problem in the true way that researchers do. You will probably have to train your TAs in how to teach such a lab to students, including how to explain background and to convey expectations for the lab. One way to increase the chances of success is to design projects so that there are several checkpoints on progress; for example, in a half-semester-long research-based lab, students could submit a brief progress report every week or two weeks so that potential problems can be addressed early. Project labs are classes in which the entire semester is built around a research project and these can be very intense integrative learning experiences for students. The CURE (Classroom Undergraduate Research Experience; *http:// www.grinnell.edu/academic/csla/assessment/cure*) survey is one tool that can be used to assess student experiences specifically in research-based courses.

> "As an example from our upper-division courses, we've recently re-organized our Department's physical chemistry curriculum, including the lab courses. The lab courses now mirror the "introductory" & "in-depth" (as opposed to "classical" / "quantum") two-semester breakdown of the lecture classes. While the first semester lab course is merely a selection of the seven most relevant (and non-overlapping) instrument-centric physical chemistry experiments that we had in the previous structure, the second-semester course is different: In the second semester the students perform a wide range of experiments (and calculations) supporting system-oriented modules — each of which lasts for several weeks. In each module, a single molecular system (or family of systems) is studied by multiple methods in an open-ended fashion (with the larger goal of answering a few main questions), allowing the students to discover what kinds of information can be learned using different approaches (and how they can complement each other to tell more of the "whole story" about a given molecular system). Some of the instrumentation used is in the physical chemistry lab, while some is in the (NMR/MS) facilities on campus, and some of the instrumentation is in the labs of individual faculty. Instead of writing traditional lab reports, students write manuscripts in journal format (or, for the last module, give a team oral presentation). The idea is to present a lab environment that is more like "real research," while also providing students with an additional pathway into undergraduate research opportunities."
> **Boyd Goodson**

> "Students engage in independent projects in both lecture and lab classes, with the latter particularly focused on following through a research proposal and obtaining results (Biological Physics lab course, our fourth-year senior lab course). The lecture class in which I have done this is Phys 344, our third-year Thermal Physics course. There, students were able to choose to present a poster on a topic related to thermal physics, e.g. a person, a concept or a device involving classical thermodynamics. Projects ranged from building heat engines, explorations of Maxwell's Demon, and biographical presentations of a physicist's life and scientific contributions."
> **Nancy Forde**

Integrating Research with Teaching

It can be both fun and profitable to integrate your research into your teaching efforts. The benefits include conveying your enthusiasm, sharing your research with students, introducing students to some of the real-world applications of what they are learning, or helping lay the groundwork for new areas. This integration can be as simple as discussing your own research when it relates to topics covered in class or specifically introducing a brief discussion of your research to let the students know about your work. If you assign research papers or proposals, some of the topics could be related to your own research. You could even develop a discovery-based laboratory related to your research, but make sure you are not depending on this for critical results. Having a TA with an interest in the outcome of the lab will also help with effective implementation. Such efforts can pay off both in the insights you might gain and in helping you recruit interested, motivated students to your group.

An important point here is that (perhaps surprisingly!) many students do not have good search strategies for finding information and do not have the skills to evaluate information they find online; the first answer is often the one that students will accept, though as we all know, it is not necessarily the best or the most accurate. If you provide a reference to a website for further reading that you have evaluated, you will ensure that students are getting good information. You might even discuss how to search for information and triage results, or even consider demonstrating your own search process.

Dealing with Resistance

Some students will resist active learning methods, often to the surprise of some faculty. But consider that lectures are comfortable and familiar. Additionally, active learning demands more of students during class and is more work for them in general. Some students appreciate and enjoy being challenged, but others may resist the extra effort required on their part and want only to sit and be passive learners. We recommend the strategy mentioned earlier of being transparent about your approach; again, explain why you are doing what you are doing, and what you hope will be gained. If you encounter resistance to innovations in teaching by students (or even colleagues), approach this like the scientist that you are and be prepared to collect data on student attitudes as well as their learning. Other strategies that people have found useful are to lead by example and to talk up potential advantages as well as to be persistent and positive about the possibility of change.

> "Lead by example. When techniques work, people take notice. However, don't only rely on teaching evaluations. Collect the data that demonstrates student learning and share it with your colleagues as well as your students. Student satisfaction is not the only important criterion. We don't hire personal trainers because it is fun to

go to the gym. We hire them because they motivate us to perform beyond what we would do on our own. It may not be fun at the time and it is often hard work, but, it is the results that matter — whether it is learning in the classroom or becoming stronger through the help of a trainer."
Andrew Feig

"I really haven't had major problems in this particular area. When I wanted to do something different, I just kept talking about it and voicing the potential advantages. I was persistent but always positive. To be fair, I've had it lucky, as my colleagues have been every bit as likely as myself to suggest new approaches, and we try to work together to bring about the best possible result. More often (at least for me) the hard part is actually making the change happen. Whether it's obtaining resources for improvements to upper-level lab courses, or gaining approval from other departments (or administrators) for lower-level courses that include non-major students, gaining support and approval from within one's own department can be the easy part. Finally, I would note that just because you've succeeded in getting a change implemented, it doesn't mean that future budget pressures won't work against you to return to the previous status quo. Perhaps not surprisingly, we've recently found that the best protection against this kind of pressure is data from ongoing assessment. In one case, we were recently able to show that students participating in a new course design had significantly better outcomes than students who did not participate; these types of fact-based arguments can be persuasive when your innovations are threatened by credit-hour bean-counting or other types of financial pressures."
Boyd Goodson

"It's hard to argue with someone who's well prepared. Prepare the material and make clear arguments for why you want to do things the way you do. I find that students appreciate that you're giving thought to your approach, even if they disagree. I don't have much experience getting colleagues to adopt new approaches, but generally I think most faculty will go along if they think that it will make their job easier, so focus on providing adequate support and making it easy."
J. Steven Dodge

Try to incorporate these methods in your courses seamlessly. For example, rather than say, "OK, now we're going to do Think-Pair-Share. First, Think about this problem. Then, form a Pair with your neighbor....", instead tell your class, "Take a few minutes to think about this and then discuss with your neighbor. After 2-3 minutes, we'll talk about your discussions as a class." This will make your efforts seem less gimmicky or contrived and far more natural, achieving the end goal desired.

4

Teaching with Technology

Should you use technology? If so, how much or how often should technology be used in your classes? In general, you should use technology when you think it will directly help students learn or will help motivate students to learn. Problems with technology during class can be very distracting, and if student grades depend on use of technology (for example, with clickers or online assignments), technical problems can engender much student angst and anger. It is critical that if you do implement technology, do not let it limit your flexibility or get in the way of your teaching. Additionally, some technologies can be quite expensive, for the institution or the student. Because different systems may be incompatible and technical support may be limited, it pays to ask around for advice about specific technologies. Use of technology is generally facilitated by well-equipped classrooms, although this is usually not absolutely necessary. For example, some classrooms are equipped with clicker receivers; however, some types of clickers can communicate through a USB receiver so a specially-equipped classroom is not needed.

Many instructors are using lecture capture technology, in which voice is synced with visual materials and then made available for later reference by students; others record and post Podcasts for students. These can be recorded during class or in a separate event. It may be somewhat time-consuming to make and post the recordings, but the availability of such materials can save time because students can answer their own questions by going back to the recordings. Such recordings can also improve student learning by saving class time for more in-depth discussions. Similarly, class wikis can make class time more efficient by dealing with questions and mundane issues in real time.

Some instructors use Facebook, instant messaging, or even Twitter to facilitate student questions and discussion. Another option is Piazza, which allows for student discussion as well as the insertion of formulas and symbols. It is worth surveying students to find out the best way to facilitate communication.

> "I approach teaching, like every other part of my job, from an experimental point of view. The first time I taught sophomore organic chemistry, it was all I could do to prepare good lecture notes, write quizzes and exams, and hang on to my sanity. But once I had the general structure of the course down, with a solid set of notes prepared, I had the time and mental space to start tweaking the course. Every year the course is a little different from the year before, and I keep the changes that seem to have worked well. I began using Instant Messenger pretty early in my teaching career to supplement office hours. A few years ago, I noticed that the number of people who would contact me by IM was considerably lower than in previous years, and found out from my grad students that "nobody uses AIM [instant messenger] any more, everyone uses Facebook." So I started using Facebook to answer students' questions in a publicly accessible forum. This became wildly popular and has taken on a life of its own. By the end of the semester, my students are using the class Facebook page to set up study groups, answer each other's questions, and chatter about chemistry-related but class-irrelevant news stories. It's been really rewarding, and it also has the added benefit of cutting down dramatically on the number of individual emails I get from the class."
> **Anonymous**

Online homework and quizzes, especially in large classes, can allow extensive data analysis to determine where specific students or the entire class needs additional instruction. Some publishers provide online homework with textbooks, saving you the effort of developing the content. Clickers can provide the same advantage in real time. Some online homework systems will allow multiple instructors and TAs to access homework data and track student progress. Similarly, standardized exams can provide the opportunity for extensive analysis of the types of problems with which students or subsets of students struggle. Computer-based problem-solving sessions led by TAs can be particularly helpful for students.

> "For introductory chemistry, our department (not just me) has recently instituted a number of changes, including:
> • Mandatory 1-credit computer workshop course, where students work on computer-based problem sets in small classes under close supervision of hand-picked TAs.
> • Clickers (which we use for real-time assessment, but which also provide the added bonus of taking attendance).
> • The introduction of an additional Honors section of the course, taught at an accelerated pace but also delving more deeply into certain parts of the material. We also 'liven up' the material by presenting 'vignettes' at the beginning of some lectures entitled "great moments in chemistry-relevant research" (from which students must select final essay topics in order to receive honors credit). This course is for chemistry majors and high-performing science majors only.
> • These changes are assessed yearly in aggregate, and broken down by population."
> **Boyd Goodson**

Simulations

There are many simulations and interactive computer programs that can enhance student understanding. Simulations can enhance learning by 1) helping students visualize a process, molecule, material or reaction, 2) work through a problem, or 3) even see how a particular reaction or process might change if parameters are perturbed. Some textbooks come with DVDs or websites that provide simulations connected to particular topics. As with demonstrations, it is important for you as the instructor to consider what students should learn from their work with simulations and structure assignments or in-class activities accordingly. There should also be follow-up discussion of the results of the simulation.

Student Personal Response Systems, e.g. "Clickers"

Personal response systems generally consist of a remote-control-like device through which students register responses to questions posed by the instructor, although phones and other personal electronic devices could also be used. The responses are usually collected through an electronic device and then recorded and/or displayed with specialized software. These systems provide one way to gauge student comprehension in real time. Many universities have adopted specific systems for campus-wide use; find out the norm on your campus so that you do not make students buy multiple different clickers of different types, both from the perspective of cost and to ensure that you have reasonable technical support.

When students can clearly see how they compare to the rest of the class, it will be hard for them to accuse you of being unfair. Student accusations of unfairness generally fall along two lines: that you are evaluating them more harshly than others and that your questions are unreasonably difficult or "tricky." When clicker responses are displayed for the entire class, it will be clear how each student compares to the entire class. If you do write the occasional confusing question and you see that in the student discussion or responses, admitting that it was confusing or poorly worded and quickly and briefly apologizing will generally improve your standing with students.

There are also mobile phone-based clicker systems. While nearly all students already have phones, this approach can be risky. For one, you are inviting students to use phones during lecture, which can introduce numerous distractions. The other, more significant issue is that students might not have adequate or consistent reception in your lecture hall, in which case you will have to find another way to obtain that feedback or give the assessment.

Should clickers be used to monitor attendance or just to give feedback to students and instructors? It is less technically involved to use clickers only for feedback or for "just-in-time teaching," rather than for taking attendance or factoring into grades. Taking attendance and grading require some kind of registration system of each student's clicker and integration of the registration information into a record-keeping system, such as an online gradebook, whereas using them only for in-class problems or surveys with no credit attached to the responses generally requires no such registration. However, you may want to use clickers for attendance or grading purposes as an incentive for students to come to class and participate by answering questions. One effective way to do this without being too punitive is to offer a grace period at the beginning of the term to allow students to get used to bringing their clickers to class and used to the system, as well as offering the ability to "drop" a few days of attendance from the graded days. Some people give a specific number of points per problem or a fraction of a point for answering a question with a full point awarded for the correct answer. Unless you have the entire semester planned in advance, it is wise to normalize the total number of clicker points to some fraction of the total grade so that you are free to use as few or as many clicker questions as you like.

Many textbooks for introductory courses (especially from major publishing houses) come with clicker questions as part of the instructor materials. Even if yours does not, you may be able to acquire a set of questions from your publisher if they are available for a different text at the same level. Other sources of questions include test banks, online quizzes or homework, or STEM education journals. Writing clicker questions from scratch can be quite time consuming, although creating a good library of questions will pay off in subsequent years.

There are numerous other lower-tech methods to implement the instant or near-instant feedback feature of personal response systems. Note cards with letter choices can be handed out with the students holding up cards to indicate their answers to posed questions. This approach has the benefit of being cheap and easy; students can quickly generate a set of cards, and you do not have to rely on students remembering to bring a device to class every day. An even simpler technique is to ask students to raise a number of fingers to represent their answer to a multiple-choice question or to vote on a limited number of answers. Whatever method you use, it is often helpful to have the students discuss the question and their answers and vote again after the discussion.

eLectures

"I joined the Chemistry faculty of the University of Houston (UH) in 2008, and in Spring 2009 it was my first time teaching a large (approx. 200 students) section of our Organic Chemistry I class. Among my colleagues, this section was referred to as the "commuter section," since it met between 5:30 and 7:00 PM and since many of the enrolled students had either part- or full-time jobs and were older than typical college undergraduates. Such a student population posed several challenges: they often simply had to miss class and could not study as regularly as traditional students. In addition, many of them had either longer-than-usual college careers or have taken a break from school, and their study habits often suffered as a result.

With these challenges in mind, I decided to set up an extensive class website that could assist them in keeping up with the course material while not sacrificing their work and family obligations. In addition to uploading the usual items found on course websites — class syllabi, sample exams and quizzes, scanned lecture notes — I wanted to create a more comprehensive and interactive tool that would approximate the experience of my lectures through digitized recordings of my voice and writing. For each of these eLectures, I identified 5 –10 key concepts that I covered in an actual classroom lecture. Then, in the silence of my office, I recorded approximately 5 minute long video segments that explained each of these topics. Using a tablet computer, I could simultaneously capture both my writing and voice, and watching the resulting video looked similar to watching me lecture and write on the board; these were created using Camtasia Studio. I intentionally avoided a rather common practice in the use of tablet computers: recording my actual lectures. I had three main reasons for doing so: (a) since I lecture with chalk and board, being tethered to a tablet seemed very restrictive; (b) lectures have a lot of "dead" time — students settling into their seats, me erasing my board, answering questions about the exams or the curve, etc., and (c) a recorded lecture presented a 90-minute long video file which was difficult to navigate to an exact point of interest. With shorter segments separately recorded, students could easily find the topic they were looking for. Afterwards, I created an interface (found at www.chem3331.com > Lectures > eLectures) which allowed the students to easily email me while listening to an eLecture, post a comment or question on the course Facebook page, or click on external links of interest. These external links (mostly to Wikipedia articles) were context-sensitive; for example, when I talked about hydrocarbons, I included the links to methane, propane, petroleum, etc. (Figure 2).

The student response to this tool was overwhelmingly positive, although I still — five years into it — have a difficult time persuading all enrolled students to consistently use eLectures. Some of my colleagues at other universities recommended my website to their students. In one of the anonymous end-of-semester evaluations, a former student of mine wrote: "I have a full-time job and I am a part-time student. Prof. Miljani's online resources really aided me on days when I had to miss lecture. His online lectures are as if you are sitting right in your seat in class. He really understands the concepts and makes every attempt to break it down to a much more tolerable level."

The creation and use of this electronic resource has not been without challenges. Initial setup took an extremely long time: I estimate that for each 90 minute lecture, approximately eight hours were needed to create the eLecture equivalent. One of those hours typically went into the preparation of materials and splitting it into appropriate segments. Three hours were needed to record all of the segments, and probably another two hours were consumed by the creation of the interface; a final hour was taken up by listening and proofreading the finalized product. This time investment is needed only in the first iteration of the course (updates during the subsequent years were quite minimal), but was a huge time drain in the first year — especially for an assistant professor struggling to simultaneously get a research program going. An additional issue is being presented by the changes in technology. In early 2009, I designed this course mostly for desktop and laptop computers — ignoring, for the time, the now-ubiquitous smartphones. In 2013, this is already a problem, as eLectures make extensive use of Adobe Flash software which is being phased out of the cellphone market, because of its large energy consumption (and thus shorter battery life). Thus, it is probable that I will need to re-code some of this material in the near future to keep it widely accessible.

I recently tried to take advantage of the fact that all my lectures are available online and to instead use lecture time to answer questions and work on example problems. Therefore, I asked the students to watch eLectures before the lecture and then come to class prepared with questions and preliminary understanding of the materials. Disappointingly, less than 50% of the class did as I advised, and some justified this by the fact that listening to my lectures and to the eLectures would take too much time. So, clearly, this tool is not a panacea.

At the end, I should point out that these eLectures probably would not exist in their current form were it not for the wholehearted financial and technical support of my College and University. This help came in several forms: free tablet computer in my first semester (provided by the NSF-funded program supervised by Prof. Jaspal Subhlok of UH Computer Science), a $2,000 summer salary supplement for this technological innovation, more than 20 GB of space on our College server, and continuous help with technical glitches that occurred along the way. It was also very rewarding to receive the 2012 UH Teaching Excellence Award, a University-level distinction that specifically cited the use of instructional technology to advance student learning.

What does future hold for eLectures? I see them as a useful model for future distance education tools. As the state support for higher education continuously decreases, and student enrollment continuously increases, public universities will be hard-

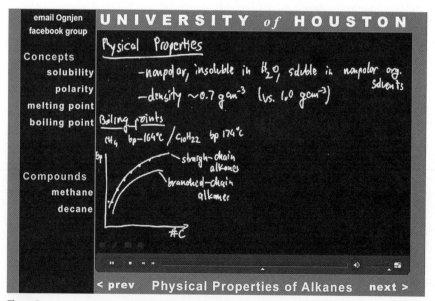

Figure 2

A screenshot of a typical eLecture. The central panel simulates the blackboard, where my real-time writing can be followed while listening to my voice explaining the concepts. The panel on the left provides hyperlinks to related concepts in other eLectures and on the web. In the top left corner, two links allow students to email the instructor, or ask a public question through the course Facebook page. Buttons on the bottom allow navigation between different concepts in the eLecture.

pressed to deliver high quality education at a low cost. To counter these trends, this and other electronic resources could be used to deliver a basic level of knowledge to an essentially unlimited audience for free. While these resources still don't come close to replacing a living person as a teacher, they may soon substitute for (overpriced) textbooks as the chief tool for the delivery of static information. In the era of smartphones, where all of the world's information is literally at our fingertips, the role of a teacher is now essentially changed from a guardian of knowledge to that of a guide through knowledge. Technology fits into this view as a vehicle to deliver raw information quickly, cheaply, and effectively over large distances; the faculty should instead focus on helping their students personalize, interpret, and apply that information to the career they see as best fitting them."

Ognjen Miljanic

Tablet PC, Electronic Inking

One of the benefits of overhead transparencies was that the instructor faced the class while writing notes. Although few of us use this technology any longer, that particular feature can be replicated by using a tablet PC or electronic inking technology. The instructor can write notes that are projected onto a screen while still making eye contact with the students or even walking around the room. The lecture outline could be a set of blank or mostly blank slides, into which movies, animations, and other multimedia features can be embedded.

"I was using an iPad as I was walking around the large classroom. The iPad was connected to my MacBookPro, where my lecture had been previously prepared with Keynote. There are a couple of advantages in walking around the classroom. First, you certainly achieve the goal of engaging the students better than by standing at the podium facing the students. As you walk around during the lecture (20 min) you get between them (hopefully, the classroom allows for that). It is important to carry a laser pointer with you as you walk around the lecture hall, as one will need it. Second, by walking around (and behind) the students, there will be less temptations from most of them to open up their laptops/tablets/phones to go on Facebook, Twitter, or shopping online during lecture. If Active Learning is the adopted approach, then lecturing while walking around the classroom really helps.

A few things that are worth considering:
1. When connecting the device, such as an iPad or iPhone, to the laptop, it is best to use Bluetooth capability. It is very reliable, whereas the connection with the WiFi can have severe shortcomings, depending on the location, type of connection, security issues, etc. I was always having trouble connecting the two devices at the beginning of the lecture with WiFi, and after I discovered the Bluetooth connection, it was perfect.
2. To run the Keynote presentation from the iPad or iPhone, the minimum required app is "Keynote Remote" (iPhone app). It is free and simple to use. It also shows the presenter's notes (although on an iPhone the screen isn't big enough to really make good use of them), and it allows one to control the presentation forward or backward, but not much else.

3. Other, much more powerful tools are "Doceri" (interactive whiteboard for iPad) and "Airserver;" when I looked around there were apps/software that also allowed one to record the lecture, but since it was the first attempt for me, I decided to keep it as simple as possible. For the next term, I will look into something more interactive, and possibly into recording the lecture. Having the ability of using the iPad as a whiteboard and marking directly on the lecture slides is a powerful capability."

Danilo Marchesini

5

Student Assignments and Assessments

Assessments are generally classified as formative, which are used to gauge student learning to adjust teaching and improve student learning on an ongoing basis, or summative, which are used to evaluate students at the end of a section or term.

Formative Assessments: Getting and Giving On-Going Feedback

Formative assessments should be used regularly to assess student learning and to adjust your teaching as needed, by reviewing material, changing your approach, or emphasizing key points. These assessments, as with summative assessments, should support your learning goals. One general feature of formative assessments is that they carry no or a small amount of credit. The goal here is to encourage participation and feedback, so some instructors give credit simply to students who participate, or give a small number of points for some assessments. Clickers and similar student response systems, described in the previous section, are often used as formative assessments, since the student responses can allow the instructor to assess student learning and make adjustments to instruction in real time.

One easy and informative assessment is to give students a few minutes at the end of a class to write a short paragraph, often referred to as the "minute paper," about the main point of the material discussed in that class period. Reading these responses will help you understand how students perceive the material and if they were able to understand and/or appreciate the main points. A similar exercise is to ask students to write briefly about what they thought was the clearest point and the least clear (i.e. "muddiest") point of the class period. This type of feedback can also be acquired through a web survey or with course management software. Concept maps can also be used in a formative manner to gauge how students view the connections between topics. We advise regular use of formative assessments to gauge student understanding throughout your classes.

Exams, Homework, and Grading

Be explicit about your grading policies. How many points are distributed to which kinds of assignments? Will late work be accepted and what are the penalties? How many points are allotted for each part of an exam or homework set? Can partial credit be given? One way to cut down on requests for regrading or arguments over points is to tell students that any request to look at an exam or assignment again will result in you going over the entire exam or assignment, which could result in actually losing points if you find an error that was in the student's favor. Others have a policy that the likely change has to be more than a certain percentage of the points to justify a regrade.

> "Exam re-dos. This seems like a cheap gag, but it is effective and a positive with students. Also, if implemented correctly, it doesn't actually affect the final grades, but it really affects how the students see you. I grade the exams quickly, within one week, then I give them a week to redo the problem they lost the most points on. They can only earn back half the points they lost. Since they cannot earn all the points back, there is not any real change to the scale, but they feel better. Further, they had a second chance to look at these problems and the concepts. It is a win-win."
> **Jenny Ross**

To save time writing exams, ask colleagues for old exams. Have students write exam questions submitted in advance, from which you pick a few to include on the exam. If you have TAs, you can also ask them to help develop exam or quiz questions, which will save you time and help in their development as educators. Another creative exam strategy is to have one "question" for which students write their own question and answer it; they are graded on the quality of the question and the response. You can do something similar in upper division courses by having students submit and then critique other students' problems before you write your exam; this process will also give you a sense of the intellectual sophistication of the class before you write your exam. Questions could be submitted in advance of an exam as a homework problem, too. One suggestion, however, is to make sure that you are responsible for the final draft of the exam itself; in addition, consider not showing the exam to your TAs in advance, as this allows them to run review sessions or other help sessions without knowledge of the exam content so that there is no chance for any unfair advantage to the students who do seek extra help from a given TA.

To be as fair as possible, grade one problem (or one page) for all of the exams at one time. If you have graders, each grader should be responsible for the same question(s) on all of the exams from the class. This way grading should be consistent from student to student and, if any particular question was unclear, it will be easier to detect. It will also be easier to determine if particular concepts are giving a large proportion of students trouble and make cheating easier to detect. To minimize bias and the effects of fatigue, grade only one problem or one page in every exam from the top of the stack to the bottom, for example from A to Z by student names, then grade the next question in all of the exams but in the reverse order, from Z to A. Use grading rubrics to define specific skills or answers that signify high/medium/low levels of competence. Devise your rubric in advance as specifically as possible: how many points for a particular part of the answer, what deduction to give for units or calculation errors, etc. It might also be of value in establishing that rubric to look through 10-15 exams on your own to see if a consistently "wrong" answer is being provided; it could be because your question was not well worded and additional answers might be worth considering for full credit as a result. Then, as you actually grade the first few exams, make notes for aspects of each answer that earn or lose points. This will help maintain consistency in grading. The same goes for problem sets; students will certainly compare marks with each other, and will be frustrated if similar (or the same) answers are not marked consistently.

In large lecture classes, multiple choice exams may be unavoidable. It may be possible to give some multiple choice questions to save time and some problems or short or long written-answer questions to make sure students can solve problems by asking them to show their work. Multiple choice questions have some benefits, in that a large amount of data is generated that can be used to determine where student misconceptions lie. However, writing good multiple choice exams is not easy; all wrong answers should be plausible without writing "trick" questions. If you find as you are grading that you have worded a question in a confusing manner based on student answers, a kind way to deal with this is to give all students all or some of the points available for that question. Online homework and quizzes and "scantron" exams are a way of dealing with large classes and have the added benefit of being able to easily determine which problems caused students the most trouble and which students are struggling with a given concept.

Asking students on a final exam to list something that they will take away from your course (for some small part of the grade, for example one-half or one percent of the exam points) can provide you with some important insights into student perceptions of your class as well as complement student course evaluations. The answers can be surprising. Similarly, you can use this mechanism to gain feedback about topics students would have liked to have discussed or things they would like to change about the course. This would not be anonymous feedback unless you structure it as such. Bonus questions are also a nice way to connect extra topics in class. A good way to use such questions is to incorporate extra topics that were presented in class, but might be slightly beyond the main scope of the evaluative components of the course, such as the year of a key discovery, or naming those who won a Nobel Prize. This might even encourage and reward classroom attendance!

Experienced instructors recommend giving many assessments to students throughout the term so that the students have plenty of opportunities to receive feedback from you. High-stakes situations in which the entire course grade rests on one or two exams are generally unpopular with students and do not encourage productive study habits or take into account events that can disrupt students' lives and ability to prepare effectively.

There are many creative strategies to encourage deeper thinking on a particular topic. Especially for upper-level classes, students can be given a figure from the primary literature and asked to provide a figure legend. Have students explain why a wrong answer is wrong. In upper-level classes especially, but also in other classes, independent research projects can be motivating, as students see the relevance of what they are learning to the real world. In laboratory classes, the focus should be on obtaining real results and can include first devising and proposing a research project that is then carried out throughout the term. Student presentations in poster or oral sessions at the end of the project can be fun for students and instructors and help students learn skills of data presentation and effective communication.

Concept inventories involve assessing student knowledge of underlying concepts. There are numerous concept inventories available for different subjects. These can be useful for assessing student learning because often students know how to solve problems but lack an understanding of the underlying concepts.

"In my upper level Biochemistry class, I have students present and critique papers from the primary literature. The first year these presentations were not very good-for one thing, enrollment was too high to allow any one student to get into too much depth, and for another, students didn't seem to know how to give talks. The next year, the class was smaller, and I gave a short introduction to what I expected from the presentations in what I thought was great detail. Yet, I found that students had a hard time implementing practices that would allow them to give an effective presentation. The next year, I gave a similarly detailed introduction, but I also required every student to meet with me the week before their presentation to go over questions and their presentation (slides and the talk). The talks were much better, and more importantly, the students learned a lot more about how to give an effective presentation. If enrollment is high, I have some students (mainly the younger students) give the presentations in pairs, so that each paper can be discussed in sufficient depth. The class gets a lot more out of the presentations, too. This approach is time-consuming, but it is completely worth it. The presentations are spread throughout the semester, so the work is distributed and fairly manageable."

Anonymous

"The first pass through my junior/senior biochemistry class was pretty rough. I had very high expectations on what the students would retain from previous courses and how much material I could cover in an hour. I felt the need to present facts for them to absorb as if that were all that teaching were. If I successfully presented them the material then of course they would learn/remember it. Class performance on the exams was abysmal (not surprising in hindsight) and the students all but rebelled because they thought their GPAs were about to be ruined. I recognized that what I was teaching would be quickly forgotten because it focused on simple factual recall more than higher order learning. So, I shifted to a very different type of course where the problems posed to the students required them to analyze data and draw conclusions, much more like what we do in the lab. The final transition was to have that process happen in class too, not just on problem sets. This led me to an interactive class where each student was given a pet protein that they would have as their own for the whole semester. It would be their example system to work on every time we did something new. In this way they got ownership of the assignment and they could compare their protein to that of their friend in the hall before class. When we talked about their protein in class, they would say something about it to everyone. It made the subject real and it made it unique for each student. It also was a lot closer to what they might do in the future in that they had to make a leap from a model system to a specific example. Most importantly, it gave them confidence in their own learning and gave them skills to look at things differently. They were not just being evaluated on learning facts and regurgitating them on exams. They could see that on the exams, they had to use the skills of data analysis they developed and it was okay not to know all of the facts. They could still get to the right answer by having that deeper conceptual understanding of the material."

Andrew Feig

Writing

"How do I know what I think until I see what I say?"
E.M. Forster

The process of writing correlates with making advances in one's own critical thinking on a topic; therefore, writing should be incorporated in classes as widely as possible. In large classes, this goal may only be feasible with well-trained TAs, either through in-class assignments or laboratory assignments. Writing-intensive assignments in laboratories can be very helpful for learning critical thinking and improving written expression skills. Writing assignments should include some aspect of revision, either in revising a particular document or expecting improvement of specific skills in subsequent written assignments throughout the term.

Grading student writing can be incredibly challenging in part because of its inherent subjectivity. There are a number of ways to save time as well as improve the quality of your feedback and therefore of student work. A few shorter assignments earlier in the term can be given in which you focus on grammar and sentence structure; these can help sharpen student writing so that later assignments should have fewer mechanical problems. More short assignments that focus on developing arguments can then be given, which will build to the ultimate assignment of a research paper or proposal. Students often arrive at college (and even graduate school) not knowing how to write a research paper, so giving them examples of papers that represent your ideal can be very helpful to them. Some online grading tools can provide canned grammar lessons and allow you to set up some standard comments; these allow you to provide fairly detailed and extensive feedback without spending too much time writing comments.

One or two rounds of peer review before you grade papers can substantially improve student work and therefore save you time in grading. Give the peer reviewers criteria on which to evaluate the work and provide some ground rules for your expectations, including guidelines for professional and respectful feedback. The extra feedback will improve the student papers you eventually get. In addition, requiring students to submit a reasonably complete draft of a paper for peer review gives them time to revise well before the final assignment deadline, independent of the review process.

6

Leading Large Lecture Classes

Although you have most likely already had a chance to teach others in a classroom setting, you have probably never taught several hundred students at once, let alone had to plan the logistics of such a class. The previous section provided insights on how to design an effective course, lessons that apply equally well to small or large courses. Thus, what we will focus on here is how to take what you already know about teaching and apply it to tackling some of the unique challenges presented by a large class environment. One particular challenge of teaching large classes, however, is that the preparation and time demands of teaching do not scale linearly.

> "One of the most difficult aspects of teaching I have encountered is facilitating the teacher — student interactions in a large class room (~150 students). I think the more the students can interact with the professor directly the better, but being at a research university, interacting with every student is impossible. In addition, even when interaction is available, not every student wants to interact with their professor for a variety of reasons. I have found that some of the students who do not put the effort into the course hide in the anonymity of a large course and are not held accountable for the grade/performance correlation. Over the last few years, I have implemented a few ways for the students to interact with me directly. I have formed groups (usually based on assignments) on online discussion boards in which the students and I can communicate. The students feel they are getting individual attention and I understand what the common misconceptions are in the assignments which I can address in class. In the biochemistry laboratory course, I replaced a few traditional lectures with group meetings (~6-10 students) to discuss data and problems encountered in the laboratory. In the biochemistry lecture, I have 20-minute discussions a few times during the semester on a reading

(focused on the scientific process) and even though only 20% of the students get to comment or speak, the classroom becomes more intimate and I can listen to the students rather than them listening to me all the time. In most of my courses, I will use a think-pair-share format using a case study and questions that ends with a few students coming to the board to show how they answered the questions. This highlights individuals and introduces accountability to the students. In addition, when the pairs are interacting, I can go around and talk to groups, providing more teacher-student contact time."

Linda Columbus

Remember, It's Entertainment

Although all excellent teaching involves some degree of entertainment to maintain students' attention and build their interest in the subject, in a large lecture class this component is perhaps one of the most critical. To maintain students' rapt attention to your presentation, whether you use chalk, a smartboard, or slides, remember that you are putting on a show, where you are the conductor. To give that concept a deeper meaning, consider that at some schools an individual student might be paying $100 per hour of instruction. With 200 students in your class, is your class actually worth $20,000? To make sure it is, have your entire lecture session planned ahead of time. For your first few classes, it might actually be worth doing a dry run. Make sure you convey confidence and stage presence, and that you project your voice sufficiently both so that people can hear you and so that you command authority. Use a microphone if it seems even remotely possible that someone in the room will not be able to hear you. Develop a sense of how large you need to write on the board for it to be visible from the back of the room. Keep in mind at the close range you will be writing on the board, it can be difficult to catch mistakes, so practice and prepare well. Although that will obviously take up time you could spend on something else (like research), a few practice sessions will help to hone your sense of timing, showing you the amount of material you can cover in a given period of time and areas where you might want to sharpen your delivery a little bit more before you go live. After a week or two of this, you will be more than ready to go live without the need to rehearse your lectures.

Now, with the mechanics covered, how do you engage the students? With 100 people or more in the audience, it can be challenging to have a lengthy discussion period or be able to answer a lot of questions on a consistent basis and still maintain control over the direction of the course and its content. Moreover, it is likely that your students will have diverse backgrounds and career goals, meaning that each is likely looking to gain different things from your course overall. Thus, your challenge is to find ways to relate the material to your students' everyday lives so you are most likely to engage them all. Have students imagine a world without the knowledge you are sharing; e.g., in an introductory course on Electricity and Magnetism, have the students speculate on how things would look without Faraday's invention of the electromagnet.

Brief discussions of the people who made key discoveries and the times in which they lived, including what was not known at the time, can also help break up the class without sacrificing too much time. Doing this in each class session will not only keep students interested, but will help to build interest in the material. Consider as well the best ways and times to use active learning techniques, such as clickers (see above), pair-and-share learning strategies (see above), and having some students work out problems on the board, to help your students stay engaged in other ways as well, and also provide you some sense of feedback on how you are doing in terms of teaching key concepts.

Moreover, show them that you care. There are several ways to do this. An obvious approach is to learn some student names. Most universities provide photographs of class members that you can look at before the first class and throughout the semester. If you learned 15-20 students from their pictures, chances are high that on that first day you could call on one of them by name. It will show your students right away that you are engaged, and that you are taking this class very seriously. As the semester goes on, and students ask you questions directly, always ask them for their name. You will never remember all of them, but it shows you are trying, and you will surprise yourself that you can probably learn 80-120 names in relatively short order. Walk around the room during class, using a wireless microphone if necessary. This accomplishes two goals: it brings you closer to students and your presence will greatly reduce non-class-related activities like web surfing or reading non-class materials. Another is to dress to impress. Sloppy clothes or things that we are comfortable wearing in a laboratory have no place in a large lecture class. Wear a tie, a sport coat or blazer, or clothes that you would wear on an interview; business casual at a minimum is a must. Students pay attention to even these minor details, at least subconsciously, and it will impact how they interact with you.

Now, how can you measure success? Classroom attendance is perhaps one of the best vehicles. If half your students are not routinely showing up, then they have perceived that your classes are not helping them with their exams, or that they can learn everything on their own without your assistance, or that perhaps you need to make your classes more engaging.

"The first time I taught a large general chemistry lecture course, I felt that I was reaching only a small subset of the students. There were 385 students in the lecture and I had a hard time engaging most of the class with a constant low background of chatter and attendance rates that hovered at 60%. I was further completely unprepared for the barrage of emails asking for special considerations for pretty much every homework, quiz, or assignment. I was teaching one of four lecture sections and I struggled to keep up with the other lecturers who had taught the course several times before. I was more focused on covering the same topics as the other lecturers (we had common exams) and did not have a clarity of purpose regarding what I wanted the students to learn. Without knowing any better, I went along with the other instructors in administering a standardized exam as the final even though the content of the exam did not very well represent concepts we had emphasized all semester. Several students recognized my good intentions but bitterly complained about the exams and my teaching evaluations were mediocre at best. Last semester I had the chance to teach the course again and I drastically modified my teaching style and the structure of the course. I insisted on being given full autonomy for my section so I would not have to coordinate with other lecturers. I drastically reduced the course content and emphasized five concepts and five critical skills I wanted students to take from the course. I reinforced some of these concepts and skills in almost every lecture. Very early on, I set the tone for interactive lecture sessions with frequent problem solving sessions and discussions and emphasizing the need to eliminate chatter. I made it a policy to not lecture more than 10 minutes at a stretch–making sure to take frequent breaks to review problems, poll the class, or show a video or animation. I made an effort to learn the names of as many students as possible and called upon them routinely. Before and after lecture, I made an effort to go into the "audience" to especially chat with students doing homework. My course syllabus clearly outlined the assessment scheme and I took great pains to review (and highlight) content before the exams and to go over common mistakes after the exams. I emphasized chemistry concepts over "trick questions" or numerically difficult questions on tests. Numerically, my teaching evaluations turned out much better, my attendance was significantly higher, and I had a large number of students asking if they could do undergraduate research under my supervision."

Anonymous

Maximizing Student Interactions Through Office Hours and Email

No matter how well you teach, students will always have questions, and one of the main challenges is how best to address them. Using email alone will likely consume far more time than you will ever imagine for a large class; moreover, many things, in fact, are difficult to explain in text without a one-on-one interaction and the ability to draw things or work out equations together. Thus, office hours, provided they are used efficiently, can limit e-mail exchanges and be one of the most useful means to provide help to students at a bare minimal expense to your own time. Here are some thoughts on how best to use your office hours:

• Hold them every week, but change their timing, as students have varied schedules and this flexibility allows for most to come to your office hours at some point or another.

• Schedule them intelligently around exams, problem sets, etc., so that students can get help at the key times they need.

• Make them group sessions. Most students have similar questions, and rather than answering the same question one at a time, twenty times total, you can do it swiftly if you have your sessions with all students who are interested. For those who really want one-on-one help, you can always offer individual appointments. Very few students will likely take you up on that offer, but they will be appreciative of it. Some of the strategies discussed above on having course wikipages, real-time feedback, and other internet-based approaches could work really well for this component.

- Consider time before and after class as extra office hours as well. Spending 15 to 20 minutes after class in particular to answer any questions will really aid student learning, and, again, pay dividends in saved time down the road.

- Be patient. Show students that all questions, no matter how basic, are worth your explanation. But, with that said, follow the advice given in the first of the Star Wars films as the Rebel Alliance is battling the Death Star: "Stay on target." Sometimes certain students may try to monopolize office hours, or ask questions that are far beyond the scope of where you want to go. These questions could be great ones, but remember that your goal is to assist the needs of the many, not the needs of just that one student. In these cases, indicate that a great question was asked, but is beyond what you want to teach, and offer to discuss the matter personally with them later on, or perhaps on a course website or discussion board. It will keep things on track, and avoid creating further confusion with students who are not at as advanced a stage and are already struggling with simpler concepts.

- Be happy to be there (or at least fake it). We all have other things to do, whether it is writing a grant, a paper, or training a researcher. But for that hour or hour-and-a-half, make sure you convey that this is the one place in the world where you WANT to be, and that you are thrilled to be answering questions. Many highly effective research scientists are not as effective in conveying that sense of excitement and commitment as one might think, and it makes students feel like an afterthought in the scheme of things.

- Explain to students that this is time you are setting aside solely for them in which you will focus your attention on their needs. Similarly, if students cannot make it to office hours, ask them to schedule an appointment rather than just dropping by, explaining to them that if they have an appointment, you will make sure your schedule is open at that time and will be ready to dedicate the time to them. Drop-ins outside of normal office hours create unnecessary disruptions and distractions for you, and so students should be encouraged to schedule appointments.

So, what about e-mail? You will certainly have to address some student questions this way. Be prompt with your answers, answer student concerns no matter what, but also be cognizant of when you are answering those e-mails. You do not want students to think you are available 24 hours a day. For instance, if you teach on the East Coast and are responding to a student query while travelling on the West Coast at 10 PM, your students will think you are available at 1 AM since that is the time stamp they will receive. In the 2-3 days before an exam, let them know the ground rules for when you will be willing to answer questions, and also let them know if you will be out of e-mail contact for some time so that they can plan accordingly as well. You might tell students that while you aim to be as prompt with your replies as possible, you generally respond to e-mail within 24 hours, or 8 business hours, or some similar set amount of time, which should also encourage them to plan ahead. To help segregate class stress from other responsibilities, consider setting up a proxy email account and put the students on notice that you will only answer email sent to that account, rather than your personal university account. You can also use TAs to screen and possibly manage class-related emails.

As noted above for office hours, often many students have the same or similar questions. One effective strategy for handling these multiple similar requests via e-mail is to copy the original question and your response from the first e-mail request on a given topic and post these on a course blog or course website that is accessible to everyone in your class. Remove any identifying information about the student and, if necessary, reword the question to make it generic. Let students know early in the term that you will do this for emailed questions and remind them to check the course website before sending you a question. Not only will this save you time, it demonstrates your commitment to fairness as you make these answers accessible to everyone in the class. This can also be a good way to show students that others often have the same questions they do. Many course management systems have a "blog" or "forum" feature where all of the students can share questions and answers. If used appropriately, these tools can dramatically cut down email traffic and allow the students to help each other.

Using Your Teaching Assistants

Hopefully, with a large class you will have some teaching assistants available, not only to grade exams and problem sets, but also to lead recitation sessions that will provide students with more help and opportunities to learn. Your teaching assistants are your first and best line of defense against mass confusion and frustration and the best support tool available for having and managing an effective course; but, to have that happen, there are definitely some things to consider.

• Messaging is important — just as in politics, you do not want one of your teaching assistants saying something that is counter to what you have taught or presented. Make sure your teaching assistants know your "talking points" by giving them your notes ahead of time, having them attend your class so they know what was taught, and making sure they understand the material well since they might have diverse undergraduate training of their own. The main reason is that from time to time, you might elect to simplify a topic, or indicate that something is not so important, and you want your teaching assistants to know that, and not contradict what you are trying to convey.

• Get feedback from your teaching assistants — since they are at the ground level, they will often hear student comments, concerns, etc., that you are unlikely to hear. Make sure you talk with assistants regularly to get their feedback. Key information can be what questions are students consistently asking, what did they have trouble with from the last lecture, etc. It will improve your lectures, and clue you in on areas where there may be broad confusion that you can address in the next class.

• Grade with your teaching assistants — any time you have a major exam where the questions are not multiple choice, spend at least 30 minutes grading with them. It will help them answer questions, provide consistency in grading, and avoid many problems down the line in terms of regrades. It also builds esprit de corps with your teaching assistants and shows them that you are invested as well in the course in ways beyond teaching itself. Again, this is taking up some of your time, but it will save you so much more down the road that the investment is well worth it.

Learn from the Efforts of Others

There are a tremendous number of resources available that can provide some insights into the concerns of students for a given course well before you ever have to teach it for the first time. Beyond end-of-the-semester evaluations, one of the more valuable, perhaps surprisingly, is a website like Rate My Professor. Although the comments there can contain vitriol and tend to reflect students on either the highly positive or negative ends of the spectrum, you will find embedded within those comments many things on their minds such as fairness, engagement with the material, teaching approaches in the past that have and have not worked in the class, etc. Simply by reading these synopses, you can glean a number of things to consider prior to designing your course at your college or university. Keep these principles in mind when reading your own (official) course evaluations. The most emphatic comments will often be at the extremes of the spectrum of opinion, and it would be unwise and unnecessarily stressful to completely redesign a course based on one negative comment. Instead, as with any type of feedback, invest most of your energy on criticisms you believe are valid and important for improvement. Brief discussions with colleagues who have taught the course before can also be invaluable.

7

Time-Saving Tips in Teaching

"Don't mistake activity for achievement."
John Wooden

As a new faculty member, time is your most valuable resource. How you manage and allocate time will determine your success to a large extent. Obviously, it is critical to be efficient and effective. Try to keep blocks of time open for research and writing by grouping meetings, teaching, etc., together as much as possible. This section will focus on a few specific tips that can help to save time, including suggestions for not reinventing teaching methods.

For nearly everything that you do in teaching and mentoring, someone will have previously done it or something similar enough to be useful. Embrace the philosophy that imitation is the sincerest form of flattery, with credit where appropriate of course. As Picasso himself once noted, "A good artist borrows, a great artist steals." Search online, use open courses/open learning initiatives, and your network of colleagues including laboratory and teaching staff at your own and other institutions to get ideas for exam and homework questions and for how to present complicated ideas, use analogies, design visual materials, carry out demonstrations, structure courses, design group projects, etc. Even if you rework much of the materials or have a different overall philosophy, having a place to start often takes less time than beginning de novo.

In addition to drawing on the memories of those who have taught your course in the past, draw on your own memories. Use your own notes from when you took the same or a similar course as a student. How was the material presented? How much was covered at once? What is not clear in your notes? Where did you have difficulty and why? What courses did you TA as a graduate student or teach as a postdoc? What active learning methods were implemented and how did they work? Having a framework in place will make it easier to experiment with your courses to accommodate different learning styles and interests.

Having an excellent textbook that contains clear, thorough explanations and complete, well-designed supplemental materials can also save tremendous time. It is hard to find the time to review many different textbooks, even if you have the authority to choose your own book. Online textbook reviews can be a good place to start, as well as talking to other faculty. Publisher representatives can also be a good resource. They want your business, so it is in their interest to give you the product that you want without wasting your time.

As is emphasized elsewhere in this document, take thorough notes the first time you teach a course. Document what worked and what you would like to do differently. Keep a schedule of what you did each day of the course and when homework, exams, and other projects were assigned and due. Keep exam and homework keys and grading rubrics. Record when labs were held and how well they correlated with lecture. Make notes on your interactions with your TAs. If there are errors in class notes, exams, or any other course materials, fix them immediately. If your grading rubrics or exams did not fully reflect your priorities, document this fact as soon as issues come up. You will almost certainly forget these details by the next time you teach the course, so having detailed notes will save you a tremendous amount of time and will help you improve the next iteration. Rewriting notes for the entire semester every time a class is taught can keep the material fresh and prompt questions to ask throughout the class. Even if you do not engage in this practice of note rewriting, a thorough review before the term and before each class will help you feel prepared and should prompt ideas for innovations in teaching. Use your teaching evaluations to identify specific suggestions and general issues that students had. Determine what students found to be effective and maintain or improve those practices. Also consider translatable knowledge; many of the impressions you have and improvements you make will transfer to other courses you will teach.

> "I took a week-long course design workshop offered through the Faculty of Education early in my career. It was team-taught by an Education Faculty member at my home institution and a physicist from another institution, and I was lucky enough to pair up with another young faculty member who had been trained as a chemist before joining the Faculty of Education. Collectively, these experts in both education and science were able to challenge my rather orthodox views on what constituted good science education. The theme of the workshop was learning objectives: what they are, how to develop them, and how to align the course activities and assessments with them to produce a coherent course design. They also discussed student-centered learning techniques that I thought were interesting but mostly unworkable in a physics classroom. I've since adopted the course design principles that I learned in this workshop to make changes both in several courses

in my department and to whole areas of our undergraduate curriculum; I have also cautiously adopted more student-centered techniques in my personal teaching habits. All of this has helped me become a better teacher, and allowed me to play a leadership role in curricular reform in our department. More recently, as chair of our graduate program, I have used design principles to develop major changes to our MSc and PhD requirements. In the next few years, I hope to help redesign the laboratory course curriculum in our department."

J. Steven Dodge

Some teaching workshops can be very helpful and can save you time. Look for hands-on workshops that involve things you need to do; for example, actually planning a new course while learning the principles of course design. Attending a teaching workshop or seminar at a professional society meeting gives you the opportunity to meet others with common goals and interests. Attend at least one at your home institution that is focused on local resources, services, and/or requirements, though recognize that these are often more general in flavor and may be targeted more globally to faculty in different disciplines, including those outside of the sciences. Backwards-design course planning, addressed above, is sometimes mentioned as a time-saving strategy because it helps you stay focused on core skills and knowledge that the students should develop rather than being distracted by trying to cover vast content areas.

"I have gradually decreased the number of "facts" in my lectures, and replaced them with letting the students interact with one another in the "process" of science. I literally teach about half the "facts" that I used to teach 20 years ago, but I think the students come out understanding better how to learn about how nature works. Anybody can look up facts now online. Putting them together in a grand pattern, organizing this pattern with a small number of models, and learning how to improve/replace these models as more facts are added to the pattern, is much harder. Among other things, this requires students even at the freshman level to always be shown how facts fit into a pattern, and how models explain the pattern. For example, I would never teach the ideal gas law equation, or how one could apply it numerically, without also deriving it from simple assumptions: the average energy per particle is the same over time, this is due to random energy exchange during collisions, but the collisions are quick enough that particles mostly move freely. These three assumptions are sufficient to derive the mathematical formula, given some definitions such as pressure=force/area, etc., that are just intuitive enough that students can be reminded of them relatively easily. Every time I finish the derivation, and the familiar formula suddenly pops up in front of them, I see their eyes widen in surprise "Oh, so I can use F=ma and random distribution of energy among particles and get PV=nRT; it's not just another 'fact,' it is an inevitable consequence of other things I know.""

Martin Gruebele

8

Identifying and Overcoming Challenges and Misconceptions in Teaching and Education

One assumption that new faculty sometimes make is that students will automatically respect them because they are faculty members. That is often far from the case, meaning that being a National Academy member or a Nobel Laureate does not lead to instant levels of awe from undergraduates. One simple way to increase respect is by dressing for the part (see above section on large lectures). In other words, dress like the professional that you are. It is also important to set expectations for classroom behavior, such as use of electronics, eating (and picking up trash), and coming and going throughout class. Are you on time? Are you ready when class begins? Are handouts and problem sets delivered on time? Are exams returned in a timely manner? Your contributions on these fronts set the overall tone.

Some students seem to think that they are invisible, that faculty do not notice what they are doing during class or even whether they are present. Most students are receptive to explanations that specific types of behavior are distracting to you and to other students. Depending on your philosophy, one approach is to explain that certain electronic devices are a distraction and must be powered off during class; however, if a student is expecting an emergency call, they must tell you before the start of the class in which they expect to need a phone. Even if you slack off on the policy later, stating it up front will send a strong message about the environment of your class. Sometimes students will ask what the consequences will be of violating policies. It can be risky to deduct points for non-academic concerns, although one solution is to have a small number of discretionary points that are for positive participation in class. Another response can be that you simply expect everyone to adhere to the stated standards of behavior.

Another common assumption is that students are like us, learn the same way that we did, are as motivated, and have as much facility with material from previous courses as most of us did. The lecture is one format that does not work well for everyone, so more variety in delivery modes, discussions, multimedia, and other ways for students to interact with material will lead to increased learning by a wider range of students. Moreover, clear lecture presentations and explanations are necessary, but are not in and of themselves sufficient for full learning. Real learning should be differentiated from information transfer and simple classroom attendance. Much student learning will occur outside of the classroom, so a role of the instructor is to direct student effort and provide feedback and structure to students, as well as to motivate them to put in the effort to learn outside of class. However, some students may still think you are not doing your job if they need to study outside of class. Other students may think that they are not smart enough if the material does not come naturally to them and they need to spend a lot of time studying, or if they cannot learn everything they need from the textbook (especially if your course goes beyond the book). You may want to tell them that students who succeed in your classes spend an average of X hours on the material outside of class for every hour in class, which may help them recognize the importance of studying outside of class, as well as convince them that needing to study does not mean that they are not "smart."

Get a sense of where teaching and curricular issues are discussed in your department or institution. How do policy decisions that impact teaching get made and how do you address such issues in your teaching? Where do people share ideas about teaching effectively? In some departments, faculty meetings are venues for such discussions, in others this happens elsewhere, and in some, sadly, it may not happen with any frequency at all. In the latter case, you might canvass with others to try to develop such a support system.

Globally, to conclude, some faculty at research universities think or are told that teaching well does not matter, or that teaching does not matter as long as you are not awful at it, in terms of your career progression including the critical steps of tenure and promotion. This proposition is false. Although you may experience no pressure or no reward for excelling at teaching, especially if you are also a strong researcher, caring about, investing in, and being a good teacher will generally increase your status in the department and the university. Even though you may encounter colleagues who do not seem to care about learning outcomes, few people want co-workers who do not care about a major part of their job. From a practical standpoint, as we are all well aware, many research proposals now require discussion of "broader impacts" and are often rejected on the basis of a weak or otherwise insufficient pedagogical component.

Part II:
Mentoring Students at Diverse Levels in Research

9

Mentoring Goals

We asked survey respondents about their experiences mentoring personnel in their research laboratories: 100% of survey respondents had experience mentoring graduate students, 98% with postdoctoral scholars, 96% with undergraduate students, 13% with professional students (dental, pharmacy, etc.), 27% with high school teachers and 33% with high school students. Furthermore, 28% had mentored research technicians.

> "Keep students on task. Never pit students against one another. Keep expectations realistic. Be sure to dole out positive reinforcement (don't forget those pats on the back). Make sure that students have at least some idea of why they are doing what they are doing (particularly for highly focused mini-projects of limited scope). Remember that everyone makes mistakes (as the old saying goes, experience is directly proportional to the amount of destroyed equipment). Don't dismiss intra-team disagreements and issues. Particularly for undergraduates, be involved during course selection so that you can help them plan to have swaths of unassigned time during the day/week that can be devoted to lab research (checkerboard course schedules are a disaster). Don't play favorites for projects or students. Treat your students something like your grown children, as they will rely on you (and represent you) forever. That said, like your children, don't try to make them all like yourself (most won't go on to be profs, and that's just fine)."
> **Boyd Goodson**

Your success will depend in large part on how well you manage your laboratory, mentor your personnel, as well as the productivity of your staff. Although you likely had no training in this area, you will need to determine effective strategies quickly. In addition to the specific strategies discussed here, there are additional resources listed at the end of this book and in the Bibliography. Ideally, your goals for your mentees and the goals of those you are mentoring will coincide. These goals at a minimum should include becoming a creative, productive, and ethical professional scientist, generating high-quality and high-impact scientific results, and achieving access to and success in one's chosen profession. There are numerous models of effective mentoring, reflecting the wide range of aspects involved. This section will highlight some general strategies for successful mentoring. Strategies specific to each student cohort (i.e., high school students, undergraduates, graduate students, postdocs) are discussed in the sections below.

First, although it may go without saying, always interview new people whom you are considering taking into your group. As much as you need people in your group, you do not need people who will be difficult or obstructionist. In a newly established group, the first members set the tone for years to come. Request the student's resume and then interview him/her. Ask about prior research and work experience, their goals for the research experience, and their long-term and career goals. This is an opportunity to tell students about your research and gauge their level of interest and overall enthusiasm.

Be sure to maintain an up-to-date and attractive website that explains your research and provides links to publications, talks, etc. This will not only convey the sense that you are organized as a researcher, but also afford inquiring students direct familiarity with your research pursuits. When students express an interest in doing research with you, give them a manageable project that they could complete within a matter of two weeks or so, for example, "write a short piece of computer code or script," or "complete a literature survey." Some faculty suggest having a prospective graduate student give a group meeting presentation on a topic of interest to your group. This serves the dual purposes of evaluating the scientific maturity of the student and sending a message to the student that joining a group is a mutual decision to be taken seriously.

Many students find it extremely motivating to have their advisor outline a few dissertation projects (chapters) early on. Even though this may, and probably will, change, it sends a message to the students that you are thinking about their primary goal of completing their dissertation.

Keep in mind that grades may be a poor predictor of research success. Drive, motivation, curiosity, and resilience, on the other hand, are important characteristics for research excellence. While these characteristics are difficult to quantify, an interview with the student can help you assess them on this front and their overall level of motivation.

Many people will advise you to develop a single management style and to be consistent. While that is generally a good strategy, also appreciate that your style may need to change depending on the specific needs of your protégé as well as their developmental stage. Some students may require more of you or specific kinds of mentoring that other students do not.

Setting Expectations

As in the classroom, establish high expectations at the outset. This can be done via formal meetings, written documents in which expectations are clearly delineated, or both. Set expectations for effort (work hours, productivity), data management, notebooks, safety, and progress reports, if any. Become a voracious reader of primary data from all students over their entire careers with you. Even mature students often miss important trends, caveats, and controls. Furthermore, by seeing data from all students, you may find instrument problems, bad reagents, or other systematic issues that your students might miss. Make sure notebooks are being kept appropriately and data are being managed. For experimental scientists, students should be in the habit of coming to every meeting with you with their current laboratory notebook, a pen, and paper. Some students take notes about progress meetings and group meetings in their laboratory notebook; decide if you would like your students to do this.

All members of the group need to be productive, for their and your careers as well as for their sense of self. You should decide if you prefer personnel to work set hours or have flexible schedules. Further, will you calibrate your expectations to a student's goals, potential, and circumstances, or apply the same standard for everyone? In general, people appreciate flexibility; keep in mind that this is a major benefit of being a graduate student. There is also extensive research on how to manage "knowledge workers" that supports the overall philosophy of allowing workers the freedom to manage their time as they desire. Some students are unprepared for this freedom and may need guidance on how to organize their work and manage their time. Specific suggestions are found below.

Be reasonably patient, supportive, enthusiastic, and as positive as possible. Try to have realistic expectations of everyone in your group based on their developmental stage. Do not take students into your group whom you do not have time to effectively mentor. Beginning students will make mistakes. Be clear that making progress will involve making mistakes, but one should not make the same mistake a second time, and certainly not a third time. As in teaching, be clear about the reasons for your decisions. This will help students understand why you are doing things and will prepare them for leadership roles as well.

Career Mentoring

Ask your students and postdocs about their career goals when you first meet with them. Remind them that you are available to help them make decisions about their future and that they should let you know how their plans are progressing. This way, when you hear about suitable opportunities, you will be able to pass them along to your students as appropriate. During the last two years of a graduate student's career, have more formal conversations about their employment goals so that you can help the students acquire needed skills and make helpful contacts. Along the way, make sure your students are acquiring professional and career skills such as project management, communication, negotiation, and collaboration skills, and mentoring skills. Individual development plans (IDPs) are useful planning tools for students and several are available free online.

Student Presentations

Graduate students and postdocs must be sent to scientific meetings and should present their work in public as much as possible. Having an undergraduate attend a conference and present their work can be a watershed moment for them, and is of high value in pre-doctoral fellowship competitions as a feather in their hat which many do not have. Obtaining positive as well as critical feedback from researchers outside of one's own institution is critical for scientific development and can also be highly motivating. Group meetings, supergroup meetings, departmental student seminars, and conferences are all opportunities for students to present their work and receive feedback from you and others in the group in advance and from the community-at-large.

Mentoring Within the Group

Establishing an expectation for horizontal and vertical mentoring in your group can be very helpful and can save you time, as long as the information being exchanged is accurate. This means mentoring between your students of similar seniority, and between students at entirely different levels of career progression. Similarly, regular meetings with your group members can dispel inaccuracies that may have been passed along and can help keep protocol drift or sloppiness in check.

Group Environment

How do you maintain the esprit de corps of the most popular, effective labs? Keep your mission for your research in mind and share it with your group often. Write down the mission statement for your research. Share your enthusiasm for the work and for all of the projects in your group. Involve students in decision making and in running the laboratory; this can be as simple as soliciting input for major decisions at group meetings or assigning group jobs, or as potentially complicated as letting a student take the lead in managing a collaboration. Encourage student feedback about how things are done. Do not give students busywork; if mundane tasks need to be done, convey why they need to be done and try to spread that work around the lab evenly, or hire a technician or student worker for such tasks. Involve your group members in the visits of seminar speakers. And have fun! Take your group out for a meal or an event, have cake or a treat at a group meeting, or do a fundraiser together. Recognize student expertise by asking them to train others. Convey to students that the overall success of the laboratory benefits everyone in it. Have a party each time a paper is published to celebrate the group's accomplishments (not necessarily just those who authored the work).

Support your students as much as possible. Edit fellowship applications, give feedback on presentations, and nominate them for awards, both local and national/international. Take the time to listen to several practice sessions of a talk when necessary, and help them prepare for their oral qualifying exams or individual original research proposal talk to the extent allowed in your department. Help them in their job search by helping them make connections and use your network to make introductions. Send letters of recommendation promptly, within hours or days. As soon as you know one of your students will be looking for a job, if not before, start working on your reference letter. Keep a record of interactions with and accomplishments of the student that you can incorporate into your letters as illustrative examples. Tell your students when you have sent their letters; it is a simple courtesy but also conveys to them that you understand how important this is to them.

Meetings

In addition to weekly group meetings, many PIs and students find it very valuable to meet one-on-one or by project in smaller groups once a week. Some labs use group meeting time for professional development workshops, such as how to give a talk or write a CV. Another type of meeting that can be very helpful is to have a group retreat, in which an entire day or significant part of a day is reserved for presentations of projects, current problems, and future plans. A simpler version of that is a "State of the Lab" address in which the PI presents the mission of the lab and how each project supports the overall mission.

Diversity

It is human nature to want to help most those who seem most like ourselves. Remember to treat all of your students with the same level of respect and as people with valid opinions. There are many excellent resources on mentoring students and others of diverse backgrounds, some of which are listed in the Appendix, which cover issues involved in multiculturalism as well as those for whom English is a second language.

Staying Organized

Many groups find having a lab Wiki to be very useful. At a minimum, a listserv/ email list, calendar, and protocol database are essential for experimental laboratories. Some groups have adopted electronic task managers and electronic notebooks to help workers stay organized.

When to Pull the Plug on Projects?

This is possibly one of the most difficult decisions that a PI or a researcher has to face. None of us got to where we are by giving up easily; thus, it is not in our natures to give up on projects, especially those developed after extensive thought and research investment. It is often next to impossible to determine if a project is not working because of an inherent flaw in the idea or approach or if the problem is the person working on it. Some suggestions: add another person to the project who can contribute some expertise that might be missing; present the problem in a "supergroup" meeting or other "safe" venue to get a broad range of suggestions; go back to proposals you wrote to put yourself in the mindset of identifying potential problems and alternative approaches. Then consider setting a deadline by which you will make a decision about the fate of the project, and let your co-workers know about that deadline as well to try and push for a final set of useful results to aid in that decision.

Motivation Issues and Other Challenges

If a student is not working out, it is better for all involved to let the student go earlier rather than later. Try to figure out early if problems are intractable; set benchmarks for improvement, be clear about them in writing, and stick to them. Some students may thrive in other research groups, so letting them go earlier in their careers gives them plenty of time to change groups without hurting their progression too much.

> "One of my first graduate students was really struggling to get results with what I thought were relatively straightforward experiments. Nothing was working and he was frustrated. At one meeting we went through possible problems and nothing obvious seemed to be the likely culprit. He finally angrily said, "Have you ever even done this [experiment] before?!" and essentially accused me of being incompetent. I took a deep breath and asked him to tell me step by step everything he did, from putting on gloves to opening a reagent to storing the samples to analysis. About halfway through the story of carrying out the experiment, I identified the problem; he was making a trivial mistake, and one I was sure I had warned him about. As gently as I could, I pointed out the mistake, told him to try again without the mistake, and that I was sure he could get this to work. He went on to be very productive. Upon sharing this experience with my colleagues, others have told me they ask students to make a photographic or video protocol in order to identify errors in carrying out experiments."
>
> **Anonymous**

One of the skills most graduate students need to learn is to balance the competing demands on their time, including classes, teaching, research, and their personal lives. Because the demands of classes and teaching are time-sensitive and immediate, research often falls down the list of priorities in those opening months of their time as graduate students. A discussion about priorities and time management with some practical advice can be helpful and sometimes will get a student back on track. If that fails, you might want to ask the student to come to your office with a list of their commitments and demands on their time, with the offer to help them find time to make progress on their research. Usually this will send the message. If not, you might have to have a conversation with the student about why they are in graduate school.

Sometimes lack of progress, poor performance, or a bad attitude signal deeper issues. Asking open-ended questions and listening to the response can lead to understanding of what is going on. The student may not actually be able to articulate the issues, though, so be prepared to wait in silence and to ask follow-up questions. Some students deal with fear of the future by sabotaging the present; if career goals have changed or students are very unsure of what they want to do, some students react with paralysis or anger. In particular, students who did not grow up with professionals and suddenly find themselves approaching a lifestyle as a professional that is very foreign to them can feel disoriented and out of their element.

Do not ignore conflicts in the lab, letting them simmer before things boil over. Remember that most of your students are probably relatively inexperienced in dealing with conflicts in a professional setting. It will be best for all involved if you provide them with the tools to resolve conflicts on their own. You can accomplish this in part by modeling the behavior you expect of them, namely, to ask questions to establish the interests and motivations of the involved parties and try to come up with a solution that maximally satisfies everyone involved.

10

Postdoctoral Researchers

It can be difficult to attract strong postdocs to your group when you are new. You can recruit postdocs at conferences and by using your network. Ask other faculty to recommend their talented graduate students to you, or have your former mentors send you applications that they cannot act positively on themselves. Definitely interview postdoc candidates to ensure their scientific competence, their communication skills, and their ability to work with others. Always check references. One bad reference is not necessarily a deal-breaker; someone providing a reference may have a specific personality conflict or just had a bad day. On the other hand, several bad references or a refusal by the candidate to provide references are red flags.

For your new group, if possible, recruit postdoctoral researchers who can provide leadership and set good examples since it is important to set the tone for the group early on. Postdoctoral researchers can provide much more than technical expertise, especially to a new laboratory, where their perspectives can be invaluable in helping write and review your grant proposals and manuscripts and in training and mentoring students. Be aware, though, that this is a two-way street, in that postdocs should be learning new skills and new science in your group, and that you also want to establish your own group ethos, not that of the former lab where the postdoc worked. Just as earning a PhD is an intense learning experience, so should this be. Postdocs should be encouraged to write fellowship applications for their own funding; even if they are not successful, the process of writing about their projects will be valuable experience.

Postdoctoral researchers bring a set of more immediate concerns in terms of their career paths. While some postdocs pursue these positions as a way of postponing career decisions, postdoctoral appointments are temporary and this should be kept in mind. Be prepared to help postdoctoral scholars define and refine their career goals and give them the resources, personal contacts, and experiences that will help them achieve their goals. It is reasonable that they may well spend 1-3 months searching for a job, so be aware of that commitment in time up front.

11

Graduate Students

When you are a new faculty member, you are an unknown quantity to graduate students. One suggestion for recruiting graduate students is to serve on the graduate admissions committee. While this can be time-consuming, you can ensure that students who fit your needs and interests will be recruited and admitted, and you will have deep knowledge of the full range of files. Often, the personal contacts you have with students during the recruiting process can lead directly to placement in your group. You can also teach a graduate course or at least guest lecture in one, which will help demystify you. You can then explicitly tell students that you are looking for new graduate students to join your group. Develop an attractive, informative, exciting web page right away to help raise awareness of your group as soon as you sign your contract, and even try and reach out to admitted students so that you can recruit a few immediately if you did not have a chance to be part of the recruitment weekends.

Give students some flexibility and freedom to explore their own ideas along with ideas that you suggest. If students propose something to do that clearly will not work, rather than let them waste time on it or shoot it down immediately, both of which could be quite deflating, have a discussion in which you explore the idea or ask them to write up a short proposal about the idea. Either they will come to the realization on their own that the idea is a poor one, or you can then help them identify the holes in the idea. It is also possible that once the arguments are laid out, the students will have turned out to be right, or at least have a useful kernel in the idea that can be used to drive their research. The latter scenario can be a huge boost to the confidence of a junior scientist and will ineluctably help invest the student in her/his research program. Part of your role is to push students to the edge of their abilities, albeit in a positive and supportive environment, to help them develop as scientists. Even though it is often faster and easier for you to do things for your students, they need to learn on their own and to develop resourcefulness. Resist the temptation to micromanage and do things for them.

It is advised to have graduate students and postdocs work on two or three projects that are sufficiently independent that one can be picked up when another is not working or while waiting for something to happen on one project. Never pit students against each other or have them compete on the same project. On the other hand, at the same time, you must appreciate that students will graduate, and, as such, some overlap will be necessary to maintain continuity of a research project if it will not be finished on the timeline of the main student involved.

Define your expectations for successful project completion. Graduating successful PhDs will help in recruiting the next generation of bright, energetic students to your laboratory. How many papers should a PhD student from your group have? How many of them need to be first-author papers? Do they need to be completed before the defense? Who will (primarily) write the papers? Consider giving your group members manuscript templates or samples; very few graduate students know what a submitted manuscript should look like or even how to best tackle its preparation. Furthermore, few students understand the importance of precision in language when describing their work; you will need to teach them. Have them read their writing aloud to others — other students in the laboratory, or even roommates or significant others. Boss and Eckert (2006) suggest that the "House of Pain" model, in which the student is present and observes while the PI edits the student's work aloud, is one model that can be effective in training students how to write. That same precision and process goes with figure generation as well as the creation of slides for talks.

The special case of co-advising students with another faculty mentor: when this works, it is beautiful; students graduate as well-rounded students with interesting interdisciplinary projects. The students have two advisors who know them well and can provide advice and access to their networks as well as recommendation letters. However, unscrupulous students (and collaborators) can abuse this system. To keep students on track and prevent time-consuming problems, put a system in place from the beginning that clearly identifies a primary mentor. A system of regular progress reports and thesis committee meetings can be very useful for keeping students on track.

12

Undergraduate Students

The enthusiasm and fresh perspectives of undergraduates and the opportunity to have a major impact on the student are two important reasons for mentoring undergraduate researchers. The key to making such relationships work well is to make your expectations clear. Is a one semester, 10 hr per week commitment enough for a student to accomplish something and warrant the training time you and your students will provide? Does your research lend itself to longer-term commitments in order for the student to be productive? Do you expect at least one summer of full-time work from a student, and if so, how will the student be compensated? Some departments have a culture of "lab-hopping," in which students change research groups every semester. You might find this to be detrimental to your productivity — after developing a student up to the top of the learning curve, they may move on to another lab. If this is the case for you, make clear your expectations for a long-term commitment from the student a priori. Explain to them that their experience in your group will be far more fulfilling if they can develop a project to completion or near completion. Some PIs even require students to sign contracts committing themselves to one research laboratory until graduation.

Having two or three undergraduates work as a team can be a productive arrangement. Undergraduate schedules can be a challenge for conducting research, but setting up a wiki for multiple students with different schedules to communicate with each other about progress on the project is one way to deal with complicated schedules. You may also want to help undergraduates with course selection to craft a schedule that maximizes time for research. Pairing an undergraduate student with a graduate student or postdoc can be a valuable experience for both mentor and mentee. Having a "pipeline" of undergraduates where the senior ones train the newcomers can also work. Keep in mind that the graduate students and postdocs may need some guidance on how best to mentor and train the undergraduates. For summer students, try to design a project that can reach an endpoint or on which the student can make substantial progress during that limited summer period.

13

High School Students, Teachers, and Other Researchers

Some faculty find that hosting high school students or teachers in their laboratories can be very rewarding, but it also requires planning, arguably more planning than most any other group of students since the level of experience and knowledge will be the least. Again, you will likely need to be selective; be sure the people you bring into your group honor their commitments and are mature enough to respect safety guidelines and expectations with respect to data and materials. It works well to have high school teachers or students work in pairs (two students, two teachers, or a teacher and a student) and to pair them with a good graduate student or postdoc mentor who has been coached in how to guide the research project. Equally important, plan a real project for them; perhaps not something of critical importance for your overall research program to move forward, but something that will generate tangible results and contribute to your research in a substantial way. Flexibility in the project is important. A well-designed project can lead to co-authorship of the high school teachers or students on publications, which will be incredibly rewarding for all involved. Remember that both populations, high school students and teachers, may have little or no research experience, so be patient. Convey your excitement about science; this is an opportunity, especially with high school students, to educate the public about what motivates scientists and how science is done, rather than dwelling on too many subtle details and caveats.

For high school teachers in particular, find out their goals for working in your laboratory. Often their motivation is to develop curricular materials or innovations that will enrich their teaching. This may actually help you improve your own teaching, so listen to their concerns and plans. The teachers can also be a resource for other students in your group, as the teachers can talk to them about their career paths and plans. You may also host community college faculty or faculty on sabbatical; again have a discussion about their goals and plan the research and other activities in which they will engage accordingly.

With high school students, it is a good idea to have a trial period to make sure the students are mature enough and that the arrangement is a good fit for both the lab and the student. A good way to do this is to set up a "potentially-renewable" month-long trial. A summer research period provides a defined time line. Consider as well that the high school students need not work five days a week, full-time. Two or three days a week can work really well, and will offer the chance for your students doing mentoring to get some other work done while also having the fulfilling and rewarding experience of mentoring a high school student.

High school students can be intimidated by the university environment and by graduate students. Spending some time with them in the laboratory can be helpful to make them feel more comfortable. The choice of a graduate student mentor is also very important; choose someone who will be supportive. It might also work better to pair a high school student with an undergraduate researcher, who would be closer in life experience but would still have more research experience. Consider establishing a team of mentors, where students move between a different mentor each day in lab; this approach requires careful organization, but again it allows for more group participation in mentoring, and divides the labor of this critical activity so no single student is overly impacted in their ability to advance their own major research project.

Outside of high school students working directly in your lab, you might also consider other ways to engage these students by giving short presentations on your work at their schools, allowing them to visit campus for an afternoon to observe your class, or giving them a tour of your labs and demonstrating what it is that your lab does (see Section below on effective outreach). For students at the high school level, even seeing a university environment and modern research laboratory can be a deeply impactful experience.

Other Researchers

Technicians, lab managers, and other staff present unique situations. In some cases, they will be in their positions for many years to come, and in other cases, their current position is a stepping stone to other opportunities. You will need to determine the goals of each of these people and mentor them accordingly.

Part III:
Developing Effective Outreach

14
Goals of Outreach

"As part of my research program, I engage quite often with local industrial collaborators on projects both small and large. I have been drawn into several regional economic development programs that are seeking to establish a blueprint for reinventing manufacturing through an emphasis on advanced technology with a focus on materials and life sciences. I've been involved with several aspects of this planning process as well as with meeting with large multinational corporations seeking to locate research and manufacturing operations. I look upon economic development and industrial outreach as an integral part of my job both in helping the university engage better with the local community as well as a means to secure the economic future of my graduate and undergraduate students."

Anonymous

In very general terms, outreach might be defined as efforts intended to broaden and diversify the demographics of scientists, provide an entrée into research for future scientists, or any effort intended to communicate science to the broader community. Definitions and examples of outreach as well as information about the need for such activities can easily be found on professional society or governmental websites (e.g. *http://www.aps.org/programs/ outreach/guide/nsf.cfm and www.nsf.gov/pubs/2002/nsf022/bicexamples.pdf*).

On a personal level, outreach can be among the most time-intensive, but also potentially among the most rewarding, activities in which faculty will engage during their professional careers. For most junior faculty, "outreach" represents an opportunity to communicate their idealism and excitement about their new job to the non-professional world. As newly anointed professors, they are often looked upon as purveyors of wisdom and insight by the lay community, and quickly find requests for interviews, public presentations, etc., competing with other job-related time demands. At the beginning especially, prioritize your efforts and activities.

In 1997, "outreach" took on new importance when it was elevated by the NSF to be included in the second merit review criterion applied in reviewing all submitted proposals. This criterion is wholly consistent with the NSF's mission statement: "To promote the progress of science; to advance the national health, prosperity and welfare; to secure the national defense (NSF Act of 1950)." By that standard, science conducted in isolation is inconsistent with that mission statement.

> "In general, the most important impact I feel I can have with outreach is not teaching students, but helping their high school or elementary school teachers. The primary and secondary teachers often have lots of questions (some of which they are afraid to ask). As a result they themselves can have a superficial understanding of the science concepts that they are teaching. In general I think the biggest impact we can have with outreach beyond simply inspiring students is to help the teachers."
> **David Vanden Bout**

Although often regarded somewhat cynically, the most successful faculty are able to incorporate outreach seamlessly into their day jobs. Outreach to undergraduate or high school students can reap direct research benefits. Undergraduates who search out research projects as students form a self-selected, and unusually highly-motivated, cadre. Particularly in this age when computing proficiency is increasingly the standard, faculty who can establish a culture of undergraduate involvement in their labs or research groups can often immediately realize the productive science that energetic and motivated students are capable of performing. An ancillary benefit is, of course, the opportunity to demonstrate to their funding agencies that they are actively training the next cadre of scientists and academics. Outreach with the community at large not only helps to educate the public about science and the frontiers of current research, it might also even lead to philanthropy for your university, department, or research program.

Of survey respondents, 67% made presentations in public as part of their outreach activities; 62% visited science classes in their local schools; 12% volunteered on an ongoing basis at either a science museum or children's museum and 10% volunteered in such venues occasionally or as needed. In terms of hosting visiting researchers, 43% hosted high school students and 31% hosted high school teachers as laboratory researchers. The specifics of the outreach activities varied widely, including open observatory nights, teacher workshops or preparing materials for teachers, being interviewed on or working with TV programs, making a movie, giving laboratory tours to students and the public, interacting with congressional representatives, working with faculty and students at community colleges or non-PhD-granting institutions, judging science fairs, and putting on science shows and science workshops for students and the public. In general, there are nearly as many different outreach programs as there are people doing them.

Faculty partner with a wide range of people when doing outreach. In our sample, 78% of respondents involved undergraduate or graduate students in their outreach activities, 56% involved staff at their own institution, 47% involved other faculty, and 25% involved others, including teachers, museum staff, and postdocs. The National Science Foundation GK12 fellows program was cited specifically as a helpful resource. As with teaching resources, there are plenty of excellent resources online, but they are generally not centralized or organized. Several professional societies have education and outreach resources on their websites.

> "I was fortunate enough to have an excellent postdoc who was awarded an NSF American Competitiveness in Chemistry Fellowship — a program that itself includes a broader impact aspect. I was able to team up with the postdoctoral fellow to implement an outreach program that could be sustained over multiple years, and with longer lasting results. Our program brought a community college student to work in our group for 8-10 weeks in the summer — we have continued this program over three consecutive summers with an excellent record of moving students into the four-year and then PhD STEM pipeline."

Stephen Bradforth

15

Developing an Outreach Program

Although in some cases, "outreach happens," concerted efforts are often required for maximal effect. Students often (generally) need encouragement to overcome their temerity about approaching a faculty member; advertising in-class or on a local job board is, of course, the most obvious means of bringing students into the fold. Almost all colleges and universities maintain a speakers bureau or faculty expertise database, which is intended to be a first point of contact for groups or individuals outside the school to locate academics versed on the topic du jour. Most of all, faculty at all levels have multitudinous grant opportunities which are designed, in large measure, to advance their broader missions; the Cottrell Scholar program of the Research Corporation for Science Advancement, which has funded the initiative to produce and distribute this book, is a prime example. In addition, many research centers have their own outreach programs with which you may be able to partner for contacts and assistance.

> "Divide & conquer! I was successful in procuring external funding to run "Lasers in Action" workshops during the year of the laser. In the budget, I specifically included funds to hire an instructor to coordinate and run the workshops. We planned them together, but I left the running of them to her and her team of volunteers. I would love to have done this myself, but could not spare the time to run two three-hour workshops each week during the school year. They were a great success!
>
> Lasers in Action workshops were targeted at students in grade 8, as this is where optics are first extensively covered in the provincial curriculum (topics such as reflection and refraction). They were designed to introduce students to the properties of light, how it interacts with matter, what makes laser light special,

and provide many opportunities for hands-on experiments with light. Students rotated among four different workstations, which they completed in groups of two or three, and which, through hands-on activities, explored the following concepts: (1) Reflection and refraction (through simple experiments); (2) Total internal reflection; (3) Color and dispersion; (4) Reflection and refraction (directing light through an optical obstacle course). By including household items like JELLO™ in the workshop (e.g. total internal reflection within JELLO™ optical waveguides; observing light transmission through different colors of JELLO™) the workshops were designed to show how Physics concepts are not limited to fancy laboratory equipment. Although the funding opportunity arose from the International Year of the Laser, the success of our initially funded one year of workshops led to the availability of university funds to continue these workshops over the years. They have now introduced thousands of students to lasers and optics, and are an ongoing component of outreach activities in our department."

Nancy Forde

Approach your outreach as a scientist, by gathering information on what is needed and what is likely to be effective to address those needs. Find the experts who understand your intended audience and obtain their advice. If you want to go into schools, ask teachers what would be most effective. If you would like to volunteer at a museum, ask an outreach coordinator or curator what is effective, what would be valuable, and for examples of other similar activities. If you want to mentor students, familiarize yourself with the literature on effective mentoring.

The most common advice given for outreach activities is to aim your approach to the level of the audience appropriately and to keep people engaged as much as possible, including hands-on activities. Your enthusiasm and obvious love for science will go a long way toward keeping people engaged. Demonstrations with everyday household or hardware store items are an effective way to convey to the public that science is all around us and is generally applicable to their lives. Handouts can also be provided with a materials list so that activities can be replicated at home (with appropriate cautions, of course). Other examples include chemistry of cosmetics, forensic science, physics of candy, and many others. Using analogies helps to impress on the audience some of the amazing feats of nature; for example, the length of DNA contained in a cell of a given size or the force exerted by a molecular motor. Asking the audience questions throughout the activity is another way to keep them engaged and make sure they are following along; this will also help you adjust the level of your presentation accordingly.

It can be very rewarding, as well as save time, to enlist undergraduate or graduate students in your outreach efforts. Your involvement can range from consultant and perhaps provider of some funding, to participant alongside the students. This is also good experience for students, who will learn how to plan an activity and explain the science behind it. Thinking about how to explain our own work to the public is also useful for us as faculty and as mentors. Hiring part-time student employees is also cost-effective. Furthermore, lecture demonstration staff, teaching staff, public engagement offices, community outreach offices, philanthropy groups, and education departments can be extremely helpful in assisting you in planning activities and making connections to community members. Many faculty members report that interactions with younger students, ranging from elementary to high school students, or their teachers, are especially rewarding. On occasion, students have been seen to record the activities with their phones to share with parents and friends later, which is really quite exciting.

Similarly, personalize your presentations. Science is done by real people. Tell the story of the people behind the work. Tell your own story. How did you get interested in science and your field of research? What have been your biggest challenges and successes? How long did it take you to make your most recent discovery? What are the current unsolved problems that need the next generation of solutions? Your students can share what excites them about their fields. Most people find that members of the public are quite interested in what we do as scientists.

The demands on one's time notwithstanding, the most successful faculty retain their initial sense of idealism throughout their careers; for them, outreach continues to be a welcome opportunity, rather than a perfunctory afterthought on a proposal to satisfy funding agency requirements or university directives.

Effectiveness of Outreach

Having defined goals for your outreach activities can be helpful in assessing whether you are achieving those objectives. This critical task can be done with self-reporting surveys, analyzing repeat attendance, informally assessing enthusiasm and excitement at the activity, tracking publications, for example, with high school students or teachers working on your research, or tracking student outcomes (college or graduate school attendance, choice of major, employment). You may also want to enlist a professional, external evaluator for specific projects, who can help design surveys or other evaluation instruments and can assist in interpreting data and designing follow-up surveys or interventions. A university institutional data analysis office or survey design service can be a good place to start.

Part IV:
Thoughts on Becoming an Effective Teacher-Scholar

16
Balancing Responsibilities

It is crucial to understand the priorities of your institution and to allocate your limited time accordingly. Remember that time is always your limiting reagent. Know what is expected for tenure and promotion. Ask questions; you may get conflicting answers, but with increasing sample size, you should be able to determine which opinions are outliers. Take the feedback that you receive in annual and other reviews seriously and discuss it with your mentors. Do what you can to address perceived shortcomings.

That being said, you may experience interactions that are perplexing, frustrating, or worse. Conserve your mental energy for things that matter. Take what you can from negative interactions to improve yourself, your work, or your outlook, but do not take things too personally. However, if you believe that you are the subject of harassment or discrimination, keep detailed records and consider speaking to a confidential advisor.

It is recommended that you not take your assistant professor teaching leave/release all at the beginning of your appointment. Many new faculty, especially those in experimental sciences, get a one- or two-semester teaching release to get their research up and running. It is advised that you save at least one of those semesters off for later. There are many benefits to teaching early, even your first semester. First, it is often difficult to make much research progress in your first semester or first year, as you wait for equipment and recruit and train your first students; however, you could gain a lot of experience from teaching your first term and could even use that class to recruit talented research students. Another good reason to teach early is to decrease feelings of isolation. Trying to make progress in an empty laboratory can be a profoundly insulating experience.

Teaching will bring you into contact with students as well as staff and other faculty and can help make you feel more a part of the community early. This advice is obviously dependent on the field. If field work or data collection opportunities occur on a limited schedule, that may require your attention instead.

Flexibility in your teaching schedule can be very valuable. Some people find it useful to teach a double schedule one semester to have another semester off. Others find it helpful to teach summer instead of during the regular semester. It is worth asking about this type of arrangement if it would be useful to you. Find out if you are expected to demonstrate proficiency in teaching a wide range of courses or to focus on one or two different classes. Team teaching may also give you added flexibility as well as an additional mentor.

Remember to document your teaching efforts and effectiveness. You may be required to report end-of-semester student evaluations. In addition to these, keep records of other assessments of your teaching that you have carried out. Many new technologies, such as ePortfolios, make this sort of record-keeping much easier and are able to support very rich documentation.

As a new faculty member, obtaining effective mentoring is essential. It is crucial that you find mentors with whom you can work well. Your mentors must be willing to listen to your concerns and be able to provide reasonable, candid feedback. For this reason it is often helpful to have a mentor outside of your home department, in addition to a mentor within your own department and discipline. In addition to mentors within your own institution, an external mentor can be extremely valuable in providing a broader perspective on professional expectations, assistance in preparing for tenure, and professional connections and opportunities. You may be able to negotiate funds for an external mentor as part of your start-up package.

> "When our external mentoring program was established, my department chair asked me to identify someone whom I thought would be a good mentor and who is also recognized as a leader in my field. I came up with a short list and ran it by my postdoc advisor. I had switched fields between graduate school and postdoctoral training, so my postdoctoral advisor was the most appropriate person to ask. I hadn't known my external mentor very well before we set up this formal relationship, but it turned out that we had a lot in common and she has been someone I truly enjoyed getting to know. My mentor has given me some extremely valuable professional opportunities as well as advice about difficult situations. The other real value of the program was for me is to get an outsider's perspective on my progress as I was nearing tenure."
>
> **Penny Beuning**

"I found at the start of my career that advice from many people outside my department and supervisors was critical to early success. Whether from people who were just a few years ahead of me (who could tell me some of their recent stories and experiences) to more senior faculty whom I met at conferences and workshops (who had a lifetime of practical experience), seeking assistance and asking advice from these individuals dramatically aided my first few years as faculty. Now, especially when I speak with younger faculty on lecture trips or at conferences, I try and pay that advice back by offering to mentor them as well, whether on grants, papers, teaching, or the faculty experience in general. I also continue to seek advice from those beyond my experience level (including outside my institution) as I have moved up the faculty ranks into additional responsibilities outside of research and teaching."

Scott Snyder

Appendix I:
Resources for Further Reading

Ambrose, Susan, Michael W. Bridges, Michele DiPietro, Marsha C. Lovett, Marie K. Norman 2010 "How Learning Works" Jossey-Bass

Angelo, Thomas A. and K. Patricia Cross 1993 "Classroom Assessment Techniques" Jossey-Bass

Boice, Robert 2000 "Advice for New Faculty Members: Nihil Nimus" Pearson

Boss, Jeremy and Susan Eckert 2006 "Academic Scientists at Work" Springer

Handelsman, Jo, Sarah Miller and Christine Pfund 1997 "Scientific Teaching" W. H. Freeman

Handelsman, Jo, Christine Pfund, Sarah Miller Laufer, and Christine Pribbenow 2005 "Entering Mentoring" Board of Regents of the University of Wisconsin System

Mazur, Eric 1996 "Peer Instruction: A User's Manual" Addison-Wesley

Mintzes, J. J. and W. H. Leonard 2006 "Handbook of College Science Teaching" NSTA

National Academies Press 1997 "Science Teaching Reconsidered"

National Research Council (NRC) 2012 "Discipline-based Education Research" National Academy Press

Nathan, Rebekah 2006 "My Freshman Year" Penguin

Wankat, Philip C. 2001 "The Effective, Efficient Professor" Pearson

Wiggins, G. and J. McTighe 1998 "Understanding by Design" Merrill/Prentice Hall

Useful Links

"How to Write Better Tests" Indiana University, Bloomington Evaluation Services and Teaching http://www.indiana.edu/~best/write_better_tests.shtml

Council on Undergraduate Research http://www.cur.org

National Science Teachers Association http://www.nsta.org

Journal of College Science Teaching http://www.nsta.org/college/

Project Kaleidoscope http://www.aacu.org/pkal/

Center for Astronomy Education http://astronomy101.jpl.nasa.gov/

American Society for Biochemistry and Molecular Biology http://www.asbmb.org/

American Chemical Society http://www.acs.org/

Institute for Chemical Education http://ice.chem.wisc.edu/

American Physical Society *http://www.aps.org/*

Physics and Astronomy Education Communities (Open Source Physics) *http://www.compadre.org/*

Assessment: Transforming Undergraduate Education in Science, Technology, Engineering and Mathematics *http://ccliconference.org/measuring-teaching-practices/*

Mentoring

http://www.nationalpostdoc.org/competencies
http://www.rackham.umich.edu/downloads/publications/Fmentoring.pdf
http://www.rackham.umich.edu/downloads/publications/mentoring.pdf

Appendix II:
Examples of Active Learning Activities

Unit 5 Day 3 Activity – "Thinking About Solutions"
CH302
Spring 2013
VandenBout/LaBrake

Name: _____

EID: _____

A major goal for this class is for you to learn the concept of macro/micro thinking or "Thinking Like a Chemist." Thinking like a chemist is the ability to look at the macroscopic properties of a static substance or a substance undergoing a change and be able to simultaneously account for those properties on a microscopic (molecular) level. Today we will practice this skill while considering the process of dissolution. Platinum stars will be on the line.

Write your answers on a separate sheet of paper.

Consider the following two crystalline substances, sucrose (table sugar) and sodium chloride (table salt). You should have prior experience at placing each of these substances in water at room temperature.

1. Please draw/explain to the best of your ability a macroscopic description of the sugar dissolving in water and the salt dissolving in water:

Given the chemical formulae/structures, consider the microscopic properties.

$C_{12}H_{22}O_{11}$ NaCl

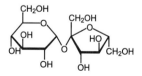

2. What type of solid is each of these substances?

3. What types of intermolecular forces hold these substances together as solids?

4. Draw a microscopic view of the dissolution process for each solid.

Check in – *if called on be prepared to share your answers with the rest of the class*

Now we are ready to look at the energy changes associated with the dissolution process.

5. Is the dissolution process an endothermic or exothermic process?

Watch a class demonstration on dissolving different compounds (sodium chloride, sucrose, and ammonium nitrate in water).

6. In general, is the dissolution process endothermic or exothermic process? *Explain:*

7. Fully describe the change in enthalpy for the dissolution process, that is what parts of the process should require energy and in what parts of the process should energy be given off.

Check in – *if called on be prepared to share your answers with the rest of the class*

8. Is the entropy of the system (pure solvent + pure solute) higher or lower after the solute has been added to the solvent and a solution has formed?

9. Is there ever a situation in which the entropy of the solvent and solute would be greater than the entropy of the solution?
Explain:

10. Is the dissolution process always spontaneous?

11. What thermodynamic property can predict the spontaneity of the dissolution process?

Check in – *if called on be prepared to share your answers with the rest of the class*

12. Thinking about the Gibb's free energy, what must be true about the enthalpy, entropy, and temperature for dissolution to be spontaneous?

Watch a class demonstration on dissolving different packing peanuts in acetone vs water.

Water (H_2O)   Acetone (CH_3COCH_3)
Standard Packing Peanuts   Bio-degradable Packing Peanuts
Polystyrene   Polysaccharide

                                        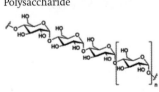

Consider the four possible combinations:
A. polystyrene packing peanuts in water
B. polystyrene packing peanuts in acetone
C. bio-degradable peanuts in water
D. bio-degradable peanuts in acetone

13. What do you think the sign is for change in free energy of solution for each of these: "+", "-" or about zero.

What do you think the sign is for change in entropy of solution for each of these: "+", "-" or about zero.

What do you think the sign is for change in enthalpy of solution for each of these: "+", "-" or about zero.

Check in – *if called on be prepared to share your answers with the rest of the class*

Unit 4 RAQ
VandenBout/LaBrake
Fall 2012

Name:

UTEID:

Consider the Following Chemical Change:

Acetylene (C_2H_2) combusts in oxygen to form carbon dioxide and water.

1. Estimate the enthalpy of combustion of acetylene using bond energies data.

Single Bond Energies (kJ/mol of bonds)						
H	C	N	O	S	F	Cl
H	436					
C	413	346				
N	391	305	163			
O	463	358	201	146		
S	347	272	–	–	226	
F	565	485	283	190	284	155
Cl	432	339	192	218	255	253	242

2. Calculate the enthalpy of combustion of one mole of C_2H_2 using heats of formation data found on the course website using your personal wireless device.

Multiple Bond Energies (kJ/mol of bonds)		
C=C 602	C=N 615	C=O 799
C=C 835	C=N 887	C=O 1072
N=N 418	O=O 498	N=N 945

3. Calculate the change in entropy for this reaction using standard molar entropy data found on the course website.

4. Calculate the change in Gibbs free energy for this reaction. Is there ever a temperature where this reaction would be non-spontaneous? If so, what is that temperature? If not, why?

5. 40 g of acetylene was combusted in a bomb calorimeter that had a heat capacity of 3.51 kJ/C for the device and contained 2000 g of water (C = 4.184 J/mol C) to absorb the heat as well. What is the expected temperature change in such a calorimeter given the complete combustion of the 40 g of the fuel.

6. What is the work for this process (combustion of 40 g C_2H_2)?

7. What is the change in internal energy for this process (combustion of 40 g C_2H_2)?

Consider the Following Physical Change:

N_2 (liq, 77K) $\longrightarrow$ N_2 (gas, 298K)

and the following thermodynamic data for N_2 :

$\Delta H^0{}_{vaporization}$ = 5.56 kJ mol^{-1}
$C(N_2 \, gas)$ = 29.1 J K^{-1}mol^{-1}

1. How much heat is absorbed during this change given 4 moles of N_2?

2. What is the work for this process (assuming the initial volume of the liquid is zero)?

3. What is the change in internal energy for this process?

4. What is the change in enthalpy for this process?

5. What is the change in entropy of the system for this process?

6. What is the change in entropy of the surrounding for this process?

7. What is the total change in entropy (change in entropy of universe) for this process?

8. Does the thermodynamic calculation predict the observation that this process is spontaneous?

Appendix III:
Use of Songs for Teaching

"Electric Field & Potential," courtesy Nancy Forde
(Sung to the tune of "Alice the Camel)"
http://www.youtube.com/watch?feature=player_detailpage&v=GpoqrvTLc8M.
(The lyrics are entirely my fault) – Nancy Forde

> The E-field flows from a ... + charge
> The E-field flows from a ... + charge
> The E-field flows from a ... + charge
> ... Go Vectors Go!
> The E-field points where the ... force goes
> The E-field points where the ... force goes
> The E-field points where the ... force goes
> ... on a POSITIVE charge
> Potential is positive 'round a ... + charge
> Potential is positive 'round a ... + charge
> Potential is positive 'round a ... + charge
> ... and negative 'round a minus

"Right-Hand Rules," courtesy Nancy Forde
(to the tune of the "Hokey-Pokey")
e.g. *http://www.youtube.com/watch?v=DkDff87CR9A;*
(The lyrics are entirely my fault) – Nancy Forde

> You put your right hand in,
> You point your thumb straight up,
> You curl your fingers around.
> (Now you've got the wire held.)
> The thumb points with the current
> And the fingers show the field.
> Charge flow produces **B** – whee!
>
> You put your right hand in
> You find the I or the v
> You point your fingers that way,
> Then you turn them to B.*
> Your thumb points where the force goes
> (if the charge is positive).
> **Force** is qv cross **B**. Whee!
> *This part can be quite tricky!

"Song: SOS"
A song about the bacterial SOS response to DNA damage, sung to ABBA's "SOS"
Sharotka M. Simon, Lauren S. Waters, Daniel F. Jarosz, and Penny J. Beuning
"Biochemistry and Molecular Biology Education" 37 316 (2009) dx.doi.
org/10.1002/bmb.20305

Appendix IV:
Survey Questions

There is currently no single, practical, and personal resource that offers advice for young faculty at research institutions on how to best develop their courses, utilize new pedagogy, develop effective outreach, and mentor students at diverse levels. Indeed, many Cottrell Scholars have identified effective strategies along these lines, but often on their own and often by "reinventing the wheel." The purpose of this survey is to gather the combined experiences and collective wisdom of 240 Cottrell Scholars to develop a book and companion website to provide advice and perspective on these issues. We are most interested in hearing about your personal experiences in developing effective teaching and mentoring practices. The text boxes below most questions will accommodate fairly lengthy answers.

This survey is anonymous and should take about 30-45 min of your time.

You will have the option at the end to identify yourself as someone willing to be contacted for follow-up discussions, in which case we may be able to link your answers to your identity. If you agree to a follow-up interview, you will still have the option to remove your identifying information from public presentations of the survey data.

1. Before you taught your first class, where did you find the most useful advice?
   Book, specify:
   Web, specify:
   Faculty mentor
   Other faculty
   Teaching workshop, specify:
   No advice or mentoring received, I was just expected to perform the first time around

2. What was the most useful advice you received before teaching your first class, or what advice might you now offer, in retrospect, to a first-time instructor?

3. After you taught your first class, what would you have wanted to change?

4. What factors are key to using technology in your classes?
   Staff support
   Technical support
   Departmental or university culture
   Other (please specify) or comments

5. What factors are hindrances to using technology in your classes?
   Lack of staff support
   Lack of technical support
   Departmental or university culture
   Other (please specify) or comments

6. What have you done or what advice do you have to overcome resistance by colleagues, teaching assistants, and/or students to adopting new teaching practices?

7. What practices do you think are most effective for motivating students to learn?

8. What advice do you have for engaging students in large lecture classes?

9. What helped you most in preparing to teach specifically a large lecture class for the first time?

10. What are examples of innovative and/or especially effective practices you have adopted in your teaching?
    Clickers/Student Response Systems
    Other non-electronic response systems (for example, cards)
    Least clear/most clear end-of-class survey
    Think-pair-share
    POGIL (Process Oriented Guided Inquiry Learning)
    Peer-Led Team Learning (PLTL)
    Creative assignments (for example, student-produced videos)
    Research experiences in teaching laboratories
    Student Assessment of their Learning Gains (SALG)
    Please describe these or other innovations you have adopted

11. What prompted you to adopt those practices?
    Desire to improve learning
    Desire to add variety to teaching
    Expectations or peer pressure
    Requirements of course or department
    Feedback from students
    Feedback from faculty or department
    Other (please specify) or comments

12. How were those innovations received by your students?
    Very enthusiastic
    Positive

Neutral
Negative
Very resistant
Comments

13. What was the biggest misconception you had to overcome in terms of teaching, campus resources on education, or anything else of significance?

14. What resources saved you tremendous time in lecture preparation, changing your pedagogy, or that you found useful more generally?

15. What, if any, impediments prevent you from implementing new teaching tools or technologies in your curriculum?
Time demands of research
Time demands of service
Teaching load
Family or other external commitments
Lack of reward or recognition for doing so
Other (please specify) or comments

16. What personnel have you mentored in your research laboratory?
Postdoctoral scholars
Research technician
Graduate students
Professional students
Undergraduate students
High school teachers
High school students
Other (please specify)

17. If you have had high school teachers or students, what advice do you have for effective mentoring?

18. Please share any advice you have for mentoring students in your research.

19. What outreach activities are you, or have you been, engaged in?
Hosting high school students as laboratory researchers
Hosting high school teachers as laboratory researchers
Visiting science classes in local schools
Volunteering on an ongoing basis in science museum or children's museum
Volunteering as needed in science museum or children's museum
Presentations in public

20. What practices have you found to be most effective in outreach activities?

21. How did you determine the effectiveness of your outreach efforts?

22. What resources have you utilized or are you aware that increase effectiveness and/or save you time in planning and carrying out outreach activities?
     Graduate or undergraduate students
     Staff at own institution
     Other faculty
     Other professionals (teachers, museum staff, etc)
     Websites
     Books
     Other
     Please describe examples of above:

23. What practices have you found to be most rewarding to you in outreach activities?

24. Please include a 1-2 paragraph description of what you consider your most successful teaching and/or mentoring experiences.

25. Are you willing to be contacted for further discussions?
This information is optional.
If you consent to be contacted, you may still request that your name or other identifying characteristics be removed.
     Name:
     Institution:
     Email Address:

Annotated Bibliography

Contents

General

Allen, D. and K. Tanner (2005). "Infusing Active Learning into the Large-enrollment Biology Class: Seven Strategies, from the Simple to Complex." *Cell Biology Education* **4**(4): 262-268. DOI: 10.1187/cbe.05-08-0113

The authors give overviews of several active learning strategies that can be implemented in large enrollment classes without radical change. This paper provides a good overview of these strategies for instructors seeking active learning techniques, and provides plenty of references for further reading. Strategies range from the short and simple, such as using discussion-prompting questions during lecture, to more involved approaches, such as problem-based learning and Workshop Biology.

Berk, R. A. (2005). "Survey of 12 Strategies to Measure Teaching Effectiveness." *International Journal of Teaching and Learning in Higher Education* **17**(1): 48-62. *http://www.isetl.org/ijtlhe/pdf/IJTLHE8.pdf*

Berk surveys literature to determine the effectiveness of twelve strategies for evaluating teacher effectiveness. With a bit of humor, he describes peer ratings, self-evaluation, videos, student interviews, alumni ratings, employer ratings, administrator ratings, teaching scholarship, teaching awards, learning outcome measures, and teaching portfolios. Beck then summarizes each strategy with a "bottom line" recommendation on whether the strategy should be used (one he says should be used "with extreme caution"). Additionally, he discusses if each strategy is appropriate for formative or summative evaluations.

104

Chasteen, S. V., S. J. Pollock, R. E. Pepper and K. K. Perkins (2012). "Thinking like a physicist: A multi-semester case study of junior-level electricity and magnetism." *American Journal of Physics* **80**(10): 923-930. DOI: 10.1119/1.4732528

The authors describe the implementation of several non-traditional instructional techniques into an upper-level physics course. With input from faculty and alumni, learning goals were developed for the redesigned course: mathematical sophistication, problem-solving expertise, and developing as a physicist. In addition to regular lectures, clicker questions, homework assignments, optional help sessions, and optional tutorials were added to the course. The redesigned course did not impact student performance on traditional exams compared with the traditional course. However, performance on a conceptual assessment was much improved with the redesigned course. This improved conceptual understanding suggests that the course redesign was successful in addressing the learning goals.

DeHaan, R. L. (2005). "The Impending Revolution in Undergraduate Science Education." *Journal of Science Education and Technology* **14**(2): 253-269. DOI: 10.1007/s10956-005-4425-3

In this review, the author briefly describes current research in several fields related to science education addressing student learning, the role of undergraduate research in learning, the benefits of information technology, and institutional changes necessary to improve science teaching. The author covers a broad range of topics, but does not address them in depth. This article should serve as a jumping-off point for those wishing to broaden their knowledge regarding science learning by seeking the references described in this work.

Feinstein, N. W., S. Allen and E. Jenkins (2013). "Outside the Pipeline: Reimagining Science Education for Nonscientists." *Science* **340**(6130): 314-317. DOI: 10.1126/science.1230855

This article focuses on how science educators can best serve students who will not go on to science careers – by teaching them to be "competent outsiders," or nonscientists who can thoughtfully interact with science that is relevant to their lives and communities. Important to the "competent outsider" is the ability to recognize important science, judge the validity of scientific claims, and find additional resources to understand unfamiliar concepts. These skills can be encouraged using techniques such as problem-based learning (PBL), Socio-Scientific Issue Discussions (SSID), and interest-driven student exploration. These methodologies are discussed, focusing on how each helps develop certain traits of the "competent outsider."

Granger, E. M., T. H. Bevis, Y. Saka, S. A. Southerland, V. Sampson and R. L. Tate (2012). "The Efficacy of Student-Centered Instruction in Supporting Science Learning." *Science* **338**(6103): 105-108. DOI: 10.1126/science.1223709

The paper reports on a large-scale comparison of student-centered and teacher-centered approaches to learning about space science in elementary school and found that the student-centered approach produced better learning outcomes.

Haak, D. C., J. HilleRisLambers, E. Pitre and S. Freeman (2011). "Increased structure and active learning reduce the achievement gap in introductory biology." *Science* **332**(6034): 1213-1216. DOI: 10.1021/ed084p1524

The authors investigated whether a highly structured course involving frequent practice with higher-order cognitive skills had any differential impact between disadvantaged and non-disadvantaged students. Previous work showed that using daily clicker questions, weekly practice exams, and a lecture-free format increased overall performance of students. Here, the authors compared biology students in a program for educationally or economically disadvantaged students to the general population of biology students and found that all students benefited from active learning, and disadvantaged students benefitted even more than the general population. Further, because the change to active learning increased the difficulty level of exam questions, based on Bloom's taxonomy, the better performance shows that students are actually learning more.

Halme, D. G., J. Khodor, R. Mitchell and G. C. Walker (2006). "A Small-Scale Concept-based Laboratory Component: The Best of Both Worlds." *CBE-Life Sciences Education* **5**(1): 41-51. DOI: 10.1187/cbe.05-02-0065

This paper describes a voluntary, small-scale laboratory component to accompany introductory biology at MIT following the Biology Concept Framework (BCF) (Khodor, Cell Biology Education, 2004). Several goals were articulated for the laboratory, such as making abstract concepts tangible and highlighting connections between different topics in the course. To achieve these goals, a combination of hands-on and minds-on activities were developed. The students who volunteered reported high expectations of the laboratory, but that these expectations were met or exceeded. Additionally, the laboratory improved student learning and retention of concepts.

Handelsman, J., D. Ebert-May, R. Beichner, P. Bruns, A. Chang, R. DeHaan, J. Gentile, S. Lauffer, J. Stewart, S. M. Tilghman and W. B. Wood (2004). "Scientific Teaching." *Science* **304**(5670): 521-522. DOI: 10.1126/science.1096022

This Policy Forum piece presents an overview of ideas for implementing and supporting scientific, research-based active learning strategies, with several successful courses and programs briefly described. Methods are introduced that can improve or even replace lectures, including the use of computer systems and inquiry-based activities. Additionally, several strategies are discussed to encourage scientists to become better teachers, such as restructuring reward systems, providing funds for new faculty to attend education workshops, and incorporating education about teaching into graduate programs. The supplemental materials, available online, provide many references for additional reading, as well as lists of online teaching resources and scientific teaching methods.

Henderson, C., M. Dancy and M. Niewiadomska-Bugaj (2012). "Use of research-based instructional strategies in introductory physics: Where do faculty leave the innovation-decision process?" *Physical Review Special Topics - Physics Education Research* **8**(2): 020104. DOI: 10.1103/PhysRevSTPER.8.020104

This paper describes the results of an online survey of physics faculty members regarding their use of research-based instructional strategies (RBIS). Respondents were asked their level of familiarity with various forms of instruction such as Peer Instruction, Workshop Physics, and Interactive Lecture Demonstrations. The study shows that 23% of faculty have used RBIS previously but no longer do so; this figure represents 1/3 of faculty who have tried RBIS. Additionally, respondents reported on twenty factors the study authors believed might influence the decision to use or continue to use RBIS, such as professional development workshops, class size, and instructor age. The study authors found that new faculty workshops were successful in introducing faculty to RBIS, but do not help the faculty continue to use RBIS. The report emphasizes that it is important to find ways to help faculty to continue using RBIS.

Khodor, J., D. G. Halme and G. C. Walker (2004). "A Hierarchical Biology Concept Framework: A Tool for Course Design." *Cell Biology Education* **3**(2): 111-121. DOI: 10.1187/cbe.03-10-0014

The authors describe the development of the Biology Concept Framework (BCF) to organize the course material from introductory biology. The BCF is hierarchical, with concepts organized by order of importance under "top-level" concepts. Additionally, concepts are cross-referenced, which is helpful for ideas that come up in multiple contexts. The article discusses motivation for and development of the BCF as well as its application.

Kind, V. (2004). "Beyond Appearances: students' misconceptions about basic chemical ideas (2nd ed.)." *School of Education*. Durham, UK, Durham University. *http://www.rsc.org/images/Misconceptions_update_tcm18-188603.pdf*

This report addresses common misconceptions about chemistry. Though it focuses on students aged 11-18, these misconceptions may carry over to undergraduates taking chemistry for the first time. The author discusses misconceptions, speculates on their origins, and presents strategies for teaching to correct these misconceptions.

Mazur, E. (2009). "Farewell, Lecture?" *Science* **323**(5910): 50-51. DOI: 10.1126/science.1168927

Wonderfully written short piece on why we should lecture less and instead guide students as they learn on their own.

Michael, J. (2006). "Where's the evidence that active learning works?" *Advances in Physiology Education* **30**(4): 159-167. DOI: 10.1152/advan.00053.2006

A review of literature on active learning techniques — includes helpful references and a list of relevant journals.

Miyake, A., L. E. Kost-Smith, N. D. Finkelstein, S. J. Pollock, G. L. Cohen and T. A. Ito (2010). "Reducing the Gender Achievement Gap in College Science: A Classroom Study of Values Affirmation." *Science* **330**(6008): 1234-1237. DOI: 10.1126/science.1195996

This paper reports on a study evaluating the use of a values affirmation activity at reducing the gender achievement gap in an introductory physics course. For the brief, 15-minute activity, each student chose from a list a value that is most important (affirmation group) or least important (control group) to the student. The student then wrote about why that value was important to them (affirmation group) or to other people (control group). The study found that the values affirmation significantly reduced the gender gap on both exam scores and conceptual understanding of physics. The study also addressed the effect of the values affirmation on those who endorse the stereotype that "men perform better than women in physics." For women, endorsement of this stereotype was negatively correlated with performance. However, this correlation was eliminated for women who completed the values affirmation. Together these results suggest that the values affirmation can address the gender gap in physics.

Modell, H. I. and J. A. Michael (1993). "Promoting Active Learning in the Life Science Classroom: Defining the Issues." *Annals of the New York Academy of Sciences* **701**: 1-7. DOI: 10.1111/j.1749-6632.1993.tb19770.x

This paper discusses several important ideas for active learning. The authors note that active learning is important for the development of problem-solving skills and appreciation of science. The role of student and teacher is different in an active learning classroom from a traditional lecture classroom, where the rationale behind each step in each activity is important. Students must be present and actively participate. The teacher must help the student learn, rather than simply disseminating information. Another important aspect of active learning is ongoing assessment to make sure students are properly prepared in addition to determining what they are learning. The authors also discuss educational objectives, learning resources, and learning environments for an active learning classroom.

Olmsted, J. (1999). "The Mid-Lecture Break: When Less Is More." *Journal of Chemical Education* **76**(4): 525-527. DOI: 10.1021/ed076p525

The use of "mid-lecture breaks" is described, a quick 2-3 minute break in lecture meant to increase student attention. These breaks allow students to recharge their brains, but also encourage student involvement. The breaks can be used for in-class assessment of material, the instructor, instructional techniques, or many other aspects of the course. Students consistently rate the mid-lecture break as their favorite aspect of the course. This method represents a simple and quick method to increase student involvement.

Riffell, S. and D. Sibley (2005). "Using web-based instruction to improve large undergraduate biology courses: An evaluation of a hybrid course format." *Computers & Education* **44**(3): 217-235. DOI: 10.1016/j.compedu.2004.01.005

A hybrid format course is compared to a traditional course. In the hybrid course, two class meetings of three each week were substituted with online homework assignments; the third class session consisted of active lectures. The hybrid course was compared to a traditionally taught course with two passive and one active lecture per week taught concurrently. The students in the hybrid course performed better than students in the traditional course. Additionally, students in the hybrid course used their textbooks much more frequently, with 80% of students reporting that they used the textbook twice a week or more.

Schearer, W. R. (1988). "Beyond the traditional lecture system of teaching chemistry: organic chemistry." *Journal of Chemical Education* **65**(2): 133-136. DOI: 10.1021/ed065p133

The paper describes how study sheets are used to improve organic chemistry lectures. The study sheets are one-page outlines of each major topic, including the major types of questions students should be able to answer and textbook problems to check understanding of the topics. Before the relevant lecture, students are expected to go through the study sheet systematically. This allows them to better understand the lecture and ask more questions. The author does not include analysis of effectiveness or student satisfaction with the study sheets, however.

Smith, A. L. and S. L. Keller (2006). "Advice for New Faculty Teaching Undergraduate Science." *Journal of Chemical Education* **83**(3): 401-406. DOI: 10.1021/ed083p401

The authors compiled advice received regarding managing time as a first year faculty member. Included are tips on choosing what courses to teach, managing time outside of the classroom, effectively creating and using a syllabus and course website, creating and grading exams and homework, and getting help from students, TAs, and colleagues.

Stassun, K. G., S. Sturm, K. Holley-Bockelmann, A. Burger, D. J. Ernst and D. Webb (2011). "The Fisk-Vanderbilt Master's-to-PhD Bridge Program: Recognizing, enlisting, and cultivating unrealized or unrecognized potential in underrepresented minority students." *American Journal of Physics* **79**(4): 374-379. DOI: 10.1119/1.3546069

The authors describe a master's program designed to increase underrepresented minority (URM) students in PhD programs. The program serves as a pipeline, but not a direct entry point for physics PhD programs and focuses on preparing URM students for success at the PhD-level. The paper describes the admission process, which focuses on student potential by such metrics as passion, motivation, drive, and leadership. Additionally, the paper describes the refinement of potential in these students through mentoring, research and presentation opportunities, and holistic skills such as time management.

Trahanovsky, W. S. (1968). "A nontraditional approach to teaching organic chemistry: The "note-test" system." *Journal of Chemical Education* **45**(8): 536. DOI: 10.1021/ed045p536

The author describes a "note-test" teaching method. In this method, students receive lecture notes prior to the start of the three-day cycle. In the first day of the cycle, the instructor covers highlights from the notes, and then opens the class for questions. The question session is continued on the second day. The third day consists of a 30-minute exam covering the material from the lecture notes, followed by discussion of the exam. Students are given hour-long lectures every 3 to 4 cycles. This method takes minimally more time than preparing lectures and covers the same amount of material, but the responsibility for learning is more clearly placed on the student.

White, H. (2011). "How to Construct a Concept Map." Retrieved July 9, 2013, from *http://www.udel.edu/chem/white/teaching/ConceptMap.html*.

This website gives a brief overview of concept maps and helpful steps for creating concept maps. Additionally, the page has several helpful links for more information on concept maps.

Wood, W. B. and K. D. Tanner (2012). "The Role of the Lecturer as Tutor: Doing What Effective Tutors Do in a Large Lecture Class." *CBE-Life Sciences Education* **11**(1): 3-9. DOI: 10.1187/cbe.11-12-0110

The authors examine the differences between learning by one-on-one tutoring or in a large lecture class. Characteristics of effective tutors are discussed, as well as implementation strategies for these characteristics. Most important, the author describes many ways for the lecturer of a large-enrollment class to translate these strategies to their classrooms.

Assessment of Student Learning

Crowe, A., C. Dirks, M. P. Wenderoth (2008). "Biology in Bloom: Implementing Bloom's Taxonomy to Enhance Student Learning in Biology." *CBE-Life Sciences Education* **7**(4): 368-381. DOI: 10.1187/cbe.08-05-0024

The authors present the Blooming Biology Tool (BBT) based on Bloom's Taxonomy to better assess biology students. The paper includes a brief overview of Bloom's Taxonomy, and then introduces the tool for use as a general guide for instructors and students. Additionally, the Bloom's-based Learning Activities for Students (BLASt) is introduced, which describes study activities geared towards each level of Bloom's Taxonomy. The authors also include three examples of very different implementations of the BBT into biology courses. In a laboratory course, students were expected to develop an NIH-style research proposal, which was graded using specific aims based on the BBT. Here, initial work on the research proposal, including collection of preliminary data, was done in groups while individual students wrote the final proposal. In a large lecture course, students were taught Bloom's Taxonomy and were expected to rank in-class questions by their Bloom's level. After exams, the instructor presented how the class performed at each level of Bloom's assessed by the exam. Additionally, students could access their individual Bloom's scores. Students were directed to BLASt to help improve their performance at each level of Bloom's. A third course using the BBT was a workshop course, where students were trained in Bloom's, then developed, answered, and critiqued their own questions at various levels of Bloom's Taxonomy.

Jacobs, L. C. December 14, (2004). "How to Write Better Tests: A Handbook for Improving Test Construction Skills." Retrieved November 27, 2013, from *http://www.indiana.edu/~best/pdf_docs/better_tests.pdf.*

This handbook offers practical advice, suggestions, and arguments for writing tests to more accurately assess students on educational objectives. Included are tips for planning the test, such as preparing a table of content and objectives (such as Bloom's levels). The bulk of the handbook is devoted to test formats, starting with how to consider what is being measured, class size, and time available when choosing test formats. Several test formats are discussed in detail – essay, multiple choice, true-false, matching, and completion. Strengths and weaknesses of several formats are discussed, as well as strategies for writing and scoring these formats. Additionally, strategies for writing essay and multiple choice questions at different Bloom's levels are presented with some examples.

Klionsky, D. J. (2001). "Constructing Knowledge in the Lecture Hall." *Journal of College Science Teaching* **31**(4): 246. *http://www.nsta.org/store/product_detail.* aspx?id=10.2505/4/jcst01_031_04_246.

See Homework *Section*

Lemons, P. P. and J. D. Lemons (2013). "Questions for Assessing Higher-Order Cognitive Skills: It's Not Just Bloom's." *CBE-Life Sciences Education* **12**(1): 47-58. DOI: 10.1187/cbe.12-03-0024

The authors observed discussions regarding the use of Bloom's Taxonomy in biology to write higher-order cognition questions. While Bloom's language was often used, other ideas were used to classify questions as higher order or lower order. Difficulty, including the time required to answer the question and student experience with the question type, was often used in classifying a question. By studying biologists' views of higher-order cognition questions, the authors suggest additional research that can be done regarding these questions.

Narloch, R., C. P. Garbin, K. D. Turnage (2006). "Benefits of Prelecture Quizzes." *Teaching of Psychology* **33**(2): 109-112. DOI: 10.1207/s15328023top3302_6

Graded, in-class quizzes at the beginning of each new chapter were assessed as a tool to encourage class preparedness. Quizzes were at the knowledge level of Bloom's taxonomy, while cumulative exams were at higher levels. Results showed that the quiz sections performed better on exams, spent more time preparing for class, less time preparing for exams, and asked higher order questions in class than sections without quizzes.

Stull, J. C., D. M. Majerich, M. L. Bernacki, S. J. Varnum and J. P. Ducette (2011). "The effects of formative assesment pre-lecture online chapter quizzes and student-initiated inquiries to the instructor on academic achievement." *Education Research and Evaluation: An International Journal on Theory and Practice* **17**(4): 253-262. DOI: 10.1080/13803611.2011.621756

The authors examine the effect of formative assessment in the form of online quizzes and contact with the instructor out of class on student performance. Two sections were compared: one was taught traditionally, the experimental section used formative assessment. Online quizzes were available for each chapter; students were given immediate feedback after completing the quizzes. Additionally, student contact by email and in-person with the instructor was logged and categorized as an "administrative" or "content" based contact. Analysis of performance revealed that quiz completion correlated positively with course performance.

Williams, A. E., N. M. Aguilar-Roca, M. Tsai, M. Wong, M. M. Beaupre and D. K. O'Dowd (2011). "Assessment of Learning Gains Associated with Independent Exam Analysis in Introductory Biology." *CBE-Life Sciences Education* **10**(4): 346-356. DOI: 10.1187/cbe.11-03-0025

This paper describes a study on the effectiveness of a "learn from exam" homework activity, in which students examine a midterm question answered incorrectly by a large portion of the class. Prior to the homework activity, students are given a brief lecture on how to analyze a question. To evaluate this activity, students were assigned to evaluate two of four questions from a midterm exam; these questions were then paired with final exam questions which were identical, had a similar emphasis, or had a different emphasis. The authors observed significantly better performance on final exam questions when the students had analyzed the matched midterm question for some of the questions used. Further analysis revealed that when the emphasis of the question was the same, students answered the matched question correctly half of the time. The authors also found that if the emphasis of the final exam question was changed, the effect of the activity was diminished. Overall, this activity improves student performance in subsequent exams on similar topics. Additionally, the activity teaches students important self-regulated learning skills that can be applied to future courses.

Classroom Demonstrations

Bowen, C. W. and A. J. Phelps (1997). "Demonstration-Based Cooperative Testing in General Chemistry: A Broader Assessment-of-Learning Technique." *Journal of Chemical Education* **74**(6): 715-719. DOI: 10.1021/ed074p715

The paper discusses using classroom demonstrations as a means of assessing students. Several demonstration-based assessment activities are discussed: separate demonstration-based quizzes and exams containing demonstrations. For exams, the demonstration can be given during the exam period, and questions related to the demonstration are included in the exam. Alternatively, the demonstration can be given in advance of the exam, and students are given questions about the demonstration to work on in groups outside of class. The authors present several examples of chemistry demonstrations and questions that can be used for assessment. In a small study, the authors compared two sections of general chemistry where one section had demonstration-based questions as part of exams. The students tested using demonstrations showed better performance on concept-based questions on the concepts illustrated by demonstrations, showing that demonstration-based assessment can increase conceptual understanding.

Crouch, C., A. P. Fagen, J. P. Callan and E. Mazur (2004). "Classroom demonstrations: Learning tools or entertainment?" *American Journal of Physics* **72**(6): 835-838. DOI: 10.1119/1.1707018

The authors examined three different modes of presenting demonstrations in an introductory physics course: the demonstration followed by instructor explanation (observe), the demonstration following a chance for students to predict the outcome of the demonstration from several options (predict), or the demonstration with a chance to predict and discuss the outcome prior to the demonstration (discuss). At the end of the semester, the observe group displayed no greater understanding of the concepts presented in demonstrations compared to a control group (no demonstration). Both predict and discuss groups understood the concepts better than the control group, with only a slight improvement with the addition of the discuss component. By giving students the opportunity to predict outcomes of demonstrations, which only take an additional two minutes, students are able to better understand and retain information from demonstrations.

Cooperative Learning

Aronson, E. and S. Patnoe (2011). *Cooperation in the Classroom: The Jigsaw Method.* London, Pinter & Martin Ltd. ISBN: 1905177224

Written by the inventor of the technique (Aronson), this book describes the jigsaw technique. Jigsaw activities divide learning materials between students; each student learns his or her portion of the material and then teaches the rest of the group.

Aronson, E. (2000). "The Jigsaw Classroom: A Cooperative Learning Technique." Retrieved October 30, 2012, from *http://www.jigsaw.org/.*

This official website for the jigsaw classroom contains an overview of the technique and tips for implementation. A history of the technique is also included, as well as a list of articles related to the technique.

Bowen, C. W. (2000). "A Quantitative Literature Review of Cooperative Learning Effects on High School and College Chemistry Achievement." *Journal of Chemical Education* **77**(1): 116-119. DOI: 10.1021/ed077p116

The author performs a meta-analysis to quantitatively examine the effects of cooperative learning on high school and college chemistry outcomes. The meta-analysis allows data from studies with different designs to be summarized together, broadening the sample size and allowing for better estimates of outcomes. Summarizing 15 studies of more than 1,500 students, the meta-analysis shows an overall increase in student performance when cooperative learning techniques are used. While the broad category of cooperative learning techniques glosses over the many different techniques available, the meta-analysis provides strong evidence of a positive effect of these techniques, especially in light of the often (statistically) small effects seen in individual studies.

Burrowes, P. A. (2003). "A Student-Centered Approach to Teaching General Biology That Really Works: Lord's Constructivist Model Put to a Test." *The American Biology Teacher* **65**(7): 491-502. DOI:10.1662/0002-7685(2003)065[0491:asattg]2.0.co;2

The author compared two sections of a college biology course. A control section was taught with traditional lectures. The experimental section was taught with short, 10- to 15-minute lectures followed by group exercises. After each group exercise, a few groups present their results to the class. This allows the professor to elaborate on the results and explain any misconceptions. This process was repeated several times during the class period, and the class period ended with a quiz. Of note, student interest in biology increased considerably more in the experimental section than in the control section.

Additionally, students in the experimental section performed better on exams, particularly on questions requiring interpreting data, application of concepts, and connecting concepts. The author also discusses strategies used to keep the groups organized.

Caprio, M. W. (1993). "Cooperative Learning – The Jewel among Motivational-Teaching Techniques." *Journal of College Science Teaching* **22**(5): 279-281. ISSN-0047-231X

The paper discusses various aspects of group learning, suggesting how each aspect can help motivate students. Included are sections on forming study groups, the benefits of group projects, and group presentations of material in class.

Carroll, D. W. (1986). "Use of the Jigsaw Technique in Laboratory and Discussion Classes." *Teaching of Psychology* **13**(4): 208-210. DOI: 10.1207/s15328023top1304_9

The author describes the use of the jigsaw technique in a psychology research design laboratory course. Students undertake two research experiments: a sample experiment replicating a published study and an independent experiment. The tasks for each study are divided between members of a group. For the independent study, each group member presents an idea, then the group can choose to undertake an experiment together or each member can perform their own experiment. Overall, the course was well received by students, and rates of course completion increased with implementation of the jigsaw method.

Carroll, F. A. and J. I. Seeman (2001). "Placing Science into Its Human Context: Using Scientific Autobiography to Teach Chemistry." *Journal of Chemical Education* **78**(12): 1618-1622. DOI: 10.1021/ed078p1618

This paper describes the use of an autobiography in an undergraduate advanced organic chemistry course. The autobiography, coupled with several papers from different periods of the author's scientific career, allows students to learn chemistry concepts in depth and in context of the human experience. After covering relevant material in class, students are assigned a paper and asked to present a summary of the paper to the class. Following the presentation, the class reviews the chemistry from the paper and discusses the context of the paper in the author's career. In end-of-semester evaluations, students reported positive reactions to the method, enjoying the greater responsibility for their own learning and being able to better humanize scientific research. Though geared towards advanced undergraduate and graduate students, this method provides an opportunity for students to learn complex topics independently.

Cooper, J. L. and P. Robinson (2000). "Getting Started: Informal Small-Group Strategies in Large Classes." *New Directions for Teaching and Learning* **2000**(81): 17-24. DOI: 10.1002/tl.810

This paper describes a variety of informal small-group learning activities and their advantages. Strategies such as think-pair-share, minute paper, Quick-thinks, and concept maps are briefly described. The authors also discuss when and how small-group activities can be implemented into the classroom.

Cooper, M. M. (1995). "Cooperative Learning: An Approach for Large Enrollment Courses." *Journal of Chemical Education* **72**(2): 162-164. DOI: 10.1021/ed072p162

The author discusses the use of cooperative learning techniques in large enrollment classes. With the use of cooperative learning, students become more responsible for and involved in their own learning and can better develop higher-order thinking skills. Cooperative learning techniques have also been shown to improve student attitudes and retention rates. Practically, the author discusses forming groups and the balance of accountability between groups and individuals. Additionally, the author discusses how to introduce group work and choose group assignments. The author also addresses two common problems with cooperative learning: not covering enough material and resentment among "good" students for helping other students along.

Crouch, C. H. (1998). "PEER INSTRUCTION: An Interactive Approach for Large Lecture Classes." *Optics and Photonics News* **9**(9): 37-41. http://www.osa-opn.org/home/articles/volume_9/issue_9/features/peer_instruction_an_interactive_approach_for_larg/#.U3UaifldVik

An early paper on peer instruction, this paper presents a brief overview of the technique, including data on students taught using peer instruction compared with traditionally taught students.

Crouch, C. H. and E. Mazur (2001). "Peer Instruction: Ten years of experience and results." *American Journal of Physics* **69**(9): 970-977. DOI: 10.1119/1.1374249

The authors describe the evolution of Peer Instruction (PI) used in introductory physics courses at Harvard University. Over ten years of use in introductory physics, the authors saw consistently higher learning gains as measured by the Force Concept Inventory. Additionally, despite the de-emphasis on problem solving in lecture, students showed increased problem solving skills. The authors also describe several modifications made to PI. Web-based reading assignments replaced reading quizzes as incentive for students to read the text before class. Structured cooperative activities were added to discussion sections as well. Strategies for teaching problem solving are also discussed. The authors describe how to better motivate students through grading and class tone. ConceptTest selection is also discussed, including ideas for incorporating open-ended and quantitative problems. The authors also describe strategies for streamlining lectures to save time and ideas for motivating TAs.

Deslauriers, L., E. Schelew and C. Wieman (2011). "Improved Learning in a Large-Enrollment Physics Class." *Science* **332**(6031): 862-864. DOI: 10.1126/science.1201783

This report describes a 1-week study in a large-enrollment introductory physics course. During the study, two sections were compared: the control section was taught by an experienced professor using traditional lecture techniques and clicker questions. The experimental section was taught by a postdoctoral fellow with little teaching experience. The experimental section was designed to give students practice thinking scientifically and used clicker questions, small-group active learning tasks, and targeted instructor feedback. Both sections covered the same topics, though the experimental section covered slightly less material in all. In a test following the study, the experimental section performed significantly better (effect size of 2.5 standard deviations) than the control section. Additionally, students were more engaged in the experimental section.

Dinan, F. J. and V. A. Frydrychowski (1995). "A Team Learning Method for Organic Chemistry." *Journal of Chemical Education* **72**(5): 429-431. DOI: 10.1021/ed072p429

This paper introduces a structured approach to using small groups in organic chemistry. In this approach, groups are designed to be maximally heterogeneous regarding academic ability, race, and gender. In advance of each class, students are given learning guides, consisting of a reading assignment, problems, and a list of specific tasks students should be able to do; each guide covers material for one class period. At the beginning of each class, groups are given a chance to briefly discuss the learning guide, and then are tested on the material, both individually and as a group. Instructors were able to cover more material with this approach than with a traditional lecture approach. Students responded well to the approach, and final exam grades were improved, although the improvement was not statistically significant.

Dougherty, R. C. (1997). "Grade/Performance Contracts, Enhanced Communication, Cooperative Learning and Student Performance in Undergraduate Organic Chemistry." *Journal of Chemical Education* **74**(6): 722-726. DOI: 10.1021/ed074p722

The author describes several strategies implemented in an undergraduate organic chemistry course. The most notable of these strategies is the use of grade/study performance contracts. These contracts, which students may opt to sign or not, guarantee the student a grade of C or better in the course if certain study requirements are met, including reading the text and attending class and recitation, transcribing notes, and studying for the course for 9 hours per week. Crucial to the contract is the clause requiring the student to visit the instructor after an exam in which the student receives below a grade of 70%. In these visits, the instructor examines the contract documents, and suggests alternate study strategies that may be implemented. Compared to a traditionally taught lecture course, retention rate in the contract course was substantially higher. Additionally, students in the contract section performed better on average on the standardized ACS exam than students in the traditional section.

Dougherty, R. C., C. W. Bowen, T. Berger, W. Rees, E. K. Mellon and E. Pulliam (1995). "Cooperative Learning and Enhanced Communication: Effects on Student Performance, Retention, and Attitudes in General Chemistry." *Journal of Chemical Education* **72**(9): 793-797. DOI: 10.1021/ed072p793

This work compares cooperative learning methods using three large sections of introductory chemistry. One section used a simple but structured cooperative learning method, with communication enhanced by email. A second section used an unstructured cooperative learning method, with enhanced communication via a modified "one-minute paper." The third section served as the control and was taught as a traditional lecture course. The structured-cooperative section showed significantly higher performance and retention rates than the other two sections. The unstructured cooperative section had higher retention than the control, but lower than the structured cooperative section. This shows that even a simple cooperative learning model has significant impact on student retention and performance.

Fagen, A. P., C. H. Crouch and E. Mazur (2002). "Peer Instruction: Results from a Range of Classrooms." *The Physics Teacher* **40**(4): 206-209. *http://www4.uwm.edu/ltc/srs/faculty/docs/Mazur_Harvard_SRS.pdf*

Authors report on a survey of instructors using Peer Instruction (PI) or similar collaborative learning strategies. Instructors using PI reported higher gains on the Force Concept Inventory (FCI) than instructors teaching traditionally. The paper also addresses common challenges to peer instruction, and several solutions to each challenge. A number of survey respondents were concerned with the time investment required to develop good ConceptTests for use in PI; the authors recommend using the abundant ConceptTests available online, such as Project Galileo (galileo.harvard.edu). With the implementation of ConceptTests, some respondents reported difficulty covering enough material; the authors recommend encouraging students to learn some of the material on their own using methods such as Just-In-Time Teaching. The authors also addressed student and faculty resistance to new teaching methods.

Felder, R. M. (1996). "Active-Inductive-Cooperative Learning: An Instructional Model for Chemistry?" *Journal of Chemical Education* **73**(9): 832-836. DOI: 10.1021/ed073p832

The author describes the details of a radical redesign of five sequential chemical engineering courses to focus on cooperative learning including in-class group exercises and group homework assignments. By using cooperative learning techniques in sequential courses, students gain additional benefits in performance, attitude, and self-confidence. Though this model would require some reworking to be successful in other disciplines, the basic elements and ideas described can apply.

Freeman, S., E. O'Connor, J. W. Parks, M. Cunningham, D. Hurley, D. Haak, C. Dirks and M. P. Wenderoth (2007). "Prescribed Active Learning Increases Performance in Introductory Biology." *CBE-Life Sciences Education* **6**(2): 132-139. DOI: 10.1187/cbe.06-09-0194

The authors examined several active-learning methods in an effort to reduce failure rates in an introductory biology course. Peer-instruction techniques were used during lecture, where the use of clickers or cards was compared, and students took practice exams, either online or in study groups. In a second term, clicker questions were either graded for correctness or for participation. Overall, failure rates were reduced and exam grades were higher than in a prior class taught without peer-instruction. No statistically significant difference was observed in exam scores between cards and clickers, graded or ungraded. However, when clicker questions were graded, students performed better on the questions. Overall, this paper shows that peer-instruction can increase student performance, though the format is not as important.

Gosser, D., V. Roth, L. Gafney, J. Kampmeier, V. Strozak, P. Varma-Nelson, S. Radel and M. Weiner (1996). "Workshop Chemistry: Overcoming the Barriers to Student Success." *Chemical Educator* **1**(1): 1-17. DOI: 10.1333/s00897960002a

This article presents the details of Workshop Chemistry and includes descriptions of the first workshop courses offered, sample workshop problems, and interviews, surveys, and logs of students, undergraduate workshop leaders, and faculty involved. The Workshop Chemistry model replaces some lecture time with 2-hour problem-solving sessions consisting of a group of 6-8 students and an undergraduate peer leader. One hallmark of Workshop Chemistry is the peer leaders, who are undergraduates who have recently completed the course successfully. These leaders are better able to connect with the students because of their status as peers and, thus, in addition to guiding the problem solving sessions, can become mentors for the students.

Gosser, D. K., J. A. Kampmeier and P. Varma-Nelson (2010). "Peer-Led Team Learning: 2008 James Flack Norris Award Address." *Journal of Chemical Education* **87**(4): 374-380. DOI: 10.1021/ed800132w

This paper provides an overview of Peer-Led Team Learning (PLTL). It includes descriptions of how the authors came to develop and use PLTL as well as how the strategy was disseminated to other institutions and instructors. A brief overview of the technique describes several critical components: Workshops as an integral part of the course, careful training of peer leaders, and appropriate problems for the Workshop. A brief literature review describes successes with PLTL. In addition, the benefits of the technique for peer leaders, faculty, and institutions are described.

Gosser, D. K. and V. Roth (1998). "The Workshop Chemistry Project: Peer-Led Team-Learning." *Journal of Chemical Education* **75**(2): 185. DOI: 10.1021/ed075p185

This is the initial report on peer-led team learning (PLTL). In PLTL, a recitation section or a small amount of lecture is replaced with a 2-hour student-led workshop. These workshops are composed of groups of 6-8 students and an undergraduate peer leader, a recent successful student of the same course. Discussion of selection and training of peer leaders is included, as are various strategies for designing the workshop problems. The method has been piloted at several diverse colleges and universities, and a significant improvement in grades, retention, and student satisfaction levels were seen.

Groccia, J. E. and J. E. Miller (1996). "Collegiality in the Classroom: The Use of Peer Learning Assistants in Cooperative Learning in Introductory Biology." *Innovative Higher Education* **21**(2): 87-100. DOI: 10.1007/BF01243700

This paper describes an adjustment to a previously described (Cheetham and Miller 1990, Cheetham, Goodwin and Miller 1991; Miller, Wilkes, Cheetham and Goodwin 1993) cooperative learning method. In an intensive cooperative learning method described in previous papers, instructors found themselves overtaxed with a class of 70 students. This paper describes the addition of Peer Learning Assistant (PLAs) undergraduates, managed by the instructor, who guide small group work during and outside of class. PLAs were meant to facilitate group problem solving and help manage group dynamics. This modification was successful in reducing the instructor's workload, while simultaneously improving student performance. Additionally, students with PLAs reported higher levels of satisfaction with their group experience.

Hagen, J. P. (2000). "Cooperative Learning in Organic II. Increased Retention on a Commuter Campus." *Journal of Chemical Education* **77**(11): 1441-1444. DOI: 10.1021/ed077p1441

The author discusses implementation of several strategies to increase retention in an organic chemistry course. The author incorporates several techniques to this goal including group quizzes, testing cycles, "muddiest point" essays, and think-write-compare (TWC). The combination of strategies resulted in an increase in retention rate by 20% without a subsequent drop in average scores on the standardized ACS exam.

Hamby Towns, M. and E. R. Grant (1997). ""I believe I will go out of this class actually knowing something": Cooperative learning activities in physical chemistry." *Journal of Research in Science Teaching* **34**(8): 819-835. DOI: 10.1002/(sici)1098-2736(199710)34:8<819::aid-tea5>3.0.co;2-y

Authors describe a discussion session in a graduate-level thermodynamics course where cooperative learning activities were implemented. In small groups, students discussed questions (given in advance) for the beginning of class, then each group presented the solution to the class. Student attitudes to this format are discussed in detail and are, for the most part, positive. Students reported that the discussion sessions increased their conceptual understanding of physical chemistry. Also, the group nature of the sessions helped the students develop better interpersonal and communication skills. Additionally, some suggestions are made for improving participation of every group member, such as assigning roles to group members and using untimed activities.

Holme, T. A. (1998). "Using Interactive Anonymous Quizzes in Large Lecture General Chemistry Courses." *Journal of Chemical Education* **75**(5): 574-576. DOI: 10.1021/ed075p574

This is a precursor, of sorts, to clicker questions, using "interactive anonymous quizzes" (IAQs) where the class is given time to respond to a question posed by the instructor and rate their confidence in their answer. Peer discussion follows where students are instructed to convince their classmates that their answer is correct. A second chance to answer the question follows discussion. Overwhelmingly students respond positively to this activity, with over 95% positive outcomes for questions (which are counted as a switch to a correct answer or an increase in confidence on the second attempt to answer).

King, A. (1993). "From Sage on the Stage to Guide on the Side." *College Teaching* **41**(1): 30-35. *http://www.jstor.org/stable/27558571*

The author describes how to gradually transition from teaching by simply transmitting knowledge, as with classical lecturing, to a more constructivist mode of learning. In the constructivist view of learning, students must construct knowledge themselves by making connections with things they already know. The author presents some activities that can be incorporated easily and without taking much time away from lecture, such as think-pair-share and concept mapping. Then the author describes more formal and involved models of cooperative learning including "Guided Reciprocal Peer Questioning" and Jigsaw.

Knight, J. K. and W. B. Wood (2005). "Teaching More by Lecturing Less." *Cell Biology Education* **4**(4): 298-310. DOI: 10.1187/05-06-0082

The authors describe a redesigned biology course to incorporate more interactive teaching methods and compare the outcomes of the redesigned course with the previous, traditionally taught course. In the redesigned course, cooperative group problem solving and in-class questions (ICQs, similar to questions used in peer instruction) were interspersed throughout the class time. Additionally, undergraduate learning assistants (LAs) were used to facilitate group work. A comparison of normalized learning gains was made, based on a pretest and a posttest administered to students in both the traditional and the redesigned course. This comparison revealed that A and B students made higher learning gains in the redesigned course, while C students fared as well in either course. Student reception to the course redesign was suspicious at first, with students disliking the interactive nature of the class. However, most students reported that the course helped their learning.

Kogut, L. S. (1997). "Using Cooperative Learning to Enhance Performance in General." *Journal of Chemical Education* **74**(6): 720-722. DOI: 10.1021/ed074p720

This describes a fairly simple use of cooperative learning, where students are required to form groups that meet outside class. A comparison is made to a similar course (same material but fewer lecture hours), showing that the students performed better on similar exams when compelled to meet in groups. Positive and negative comments on the method are presented.

Lasry, N. (2008). "Clickers or Flashcards: Is There Really a Difference?" *The Physics Teacher* **46**(4): 242-244. DOI: 10.1119/1.2895678

This paper reports on a study comparing the use of clickers and flashcards in Peer Instruction (PI). No significant difference in conceptual learning gains or exam scores was found between sections using clickers or flashcards. Other differences are noted between the two systems. Using flashcards requires instructors to tabulate or estimate responses, costing class time. Clickers tabulate automatically and allow student responses to be archived. Archived responses present an opportunity to refine questions to be more effective. Additional considerations are the appeal of technology and the expense of using clickers.

Lewis, S. E. and J. E. Lewis (2005). "Departing from Lectures: An Evaluation of a Peer-Led Guided Inquiry Alternative." *Journal of Chemical Education* **82**(1): 135-139. DOI: 10.1021/ed082p135

This paper describes a combination of Peer-Led Team Learning (PLTL) and guided inquiry into a new method, Peer-Led Guided Inquiry (PLGI). The experimental section attended two regular 50-minute lectures and one 50-minute PLGI session each week, while the control section attended three 50-minute lectures each week. Exam results indicate that the experimental section consistently outperformed the control section on exams. Additionally, attendance at PLGI sessions was correlated with better performance.

Libby, R. D. (1995). "Piaget and Organic Chemistry: Teaching Introductory Organic Chemistry through Learning Cycles." *Journal of Chemical Education* **72**(7): 626-631. DOI: 10.1021/ed072p626

The author discusses implementation of learning cycles into an organic chemistry course. Learning cycles rely very little on lecture. Rather, students discover concepts themselves through the process. Prior to class, students explore a set of data using example problems then students and the instructor work together to develop a hypothesis to fit the data. Finally, students supply the hypothesis to new situations outside of class. Detailed instructions are given on developing this method for use in other classrooms. Though no data is presented, the author observes that students performed as well on standardized exams when taught by learning cycles as they did when taught using traditional lecture methods, but with better attitudes. Learning cycles provide students experience with the scientific thought processes, an additional benefit over traditional lecture.

Paulson, D. R. (1999). "Active Learning and Cooperative Learning in the Organic Chemistry Lecture Class." *Journal of Chemical Education* **76**(8): 1136-1140. DOI: 10.1021/ed076p1136

The author describes his experiences incorporating several active and cooperative learning techniques into a three-term organic chemistry sequence in order to decrease attrition rates. The author formed cooperative learning groups who worked together on activities both during and outside of class time. Students were also given one minute quizzes on assigned readings at the beginning of each class to encourage pre-class preparation. Finger signals (similar to the flashcard or clicker techniques) were used to answer in-class questions. Additionally, the "minute paper" was implemented as were guided class discussions. While the author continued to lecture as the main means of transmitting information, breaks and pauses were incorporated into lectures to increase understanding. One year of the sequence was analyzed using either a standard lecture format or the cooperative and active learning techniques. This analysis showed that the average retention rate for the full sequence increased from 38% to 75% upon incorporation of the new techniques. Though only one year of each method was compared, the results are striking and the personal nature of the report is helpful for those seeking to incorporate newer teaching methods into their lecture-based courses.

Perkins, D. V. and R. N. Saris (2001). "A "Jigsaw Classroom" Technique for Undergraduate Statistics Courses." *Teaching of Psychology* **28**(2): 111-113. DOI: 10.1207/s15328023top2802_09

The authors report on the use of the "jigsaw classroom" technique in an undergraduate statistics course. In this case, the technique was implemented in an activity using worksheets. Each activity was divided into two to four parts necessary for the final solution, and each part was distributed on a separate worksheet to a group of students. The students worked on their worksheet as a group, and then split up to find other students with different worksheets. Together, these students completed a final worksheet. In general, students responded positively to the activity, with 84% enjoying the time savings of working together on the worksheets and 88% finding the activity a positive alternative to lecture.

Poole, M. J. and R. E. Glaser (1999). "Organic Chemistry Online: Building Collaborative Learning Communities through Electronic Communication Tools." *Journal of Chemical Education* **76**(5): 699-703. DOI: 10.1021/ed076p699

This paper describes a group research project used in an undergraduate organic chemistry course. This project was implemented to develop small learning communities within the larger lecture course. The research project required students to draw heavily from internet resources, and the finished projects were published online. Students participating in this project achieved higher exam grades than students in previous years, before the group project was implemented.

Ross, M. R. and R. B. Fulton (1994). "Active Learning Strategies in the Analytical Chemistry Classroom." *Journal of Chemical Education* **71**(2): 141-143. DOI: 10.1021/ ed071p141

The author presents a redesigned course focusing on cooperative learning. Course material is broken down into three-day cycles, each covering approximately one chapter in the textbook. Students are given homework problems, due the first day of each cycle. The first day of the cycle, students work in groups on the homework problems. Over the following two class days, groups present the solutions to the problems and important concepts contained within the problem. Here, the instructor facilitates discussion and provides mini-lectures to complement the problems. Additionally, the course includes quizzes after every two cycles, and an orally administered final exam that allows the instructor to probe students more fully. Students perform as well or better than students taught in the traditional manner, and the same amount of material is covered.

Smith, M. K., W. B. Wood, W. K. Adams, C. Wieman, J. K. Knight, N. Guild and T. T. Su (2009). "Why Peer Discussion Improves Student Performance on In-Class Concept Questions." *Science* **323**(5910): 122-124. DOI: 10.1126/ science.1165919

The authors show that students improve on clicker questions after discussion with peers, even when the question following discussion is modified (but still on the same concept) from the discussed question, showing that peer discussion increases student understanding.

Tien, L. T., V. Roth and J. A. Kampmeier (2002). "Implementation of a peer-led team learning instructional approach in an undergraduate organic chemistry course." *Journal of Research in Science Teaching* **39**(7): 606-632. DOI: 10.1002/ tea.10038

The paper describes interviews with peer leaders, who have perspective as both a student and a peer leader. The excerpts from the interviews are mostly about how exciting the teaching was and the strategies they used.

Towns, M. H. (1998). "How Do I Get My Students to Work Together? Getting Cooperative Learning Started." *Journal of Chemical Education* **75**(1): 67-69. DOI: 10.1021/ed075p67

The author presents strategies for improving quality of group dynamics when using cooperative learning techniques. In order for group activities to work, groups must know how to work together and be willing to work together. The author describes how she encourages groups to work together in her classes. Students are told why they are working in groups and how the groups are being formed. "Group Covenants" are created, describing the responsibilities of each member of the group and of the group as a whole. This is an excellent resource for facilitating cooperative learning and teaching students how to work together in teams.

Watson, S. B. and J. E. Marshall (1995). "Effects of cooperative incentives and heterogeneous arrangement on achievement and interaction of cooperative learning groups in a college life science course." *Journal of Research in Science Teaching* **32**(3): 291-299. DOI: 10.1002/tea.3660320308

This paper looks at the effect of heterogeneous grouping and cooperative incentives in cooperative learning. Groups were created based on achievement on a pretest — students were either assigned to homogeneous groups with students who performed similarly on the pretest or to heterogeneous groups, with students of different performance levels. Then, the homogeneous and heterogeneous groups were assigned either cooperative and individual incentives or only individual incentives. After a posttest, no significant difference was seen between any of the groups in terms of achievement. However, heterogeneous groups were found to interact more than homogeneous groups. The authors note that these groups were assigned based on their knowledge of the current subject matter. A more comprehensive way to assign groups might include a metric of learning ability or performance, such as grades in prerequisite classes, overall GPA, or standardized test scores.

Homework

Allain, R. and T. Williams (2006). "The Effectiveness of Online Homework in an Introductory Science Class." *Journal of College Science Teaching* **35**(6): 28-30. *http://www.nsta.org/publications/news/story.aspx?id=51970*

The paper examines the use of online homework assignments on student learning. Sections with graded online homework or assigned but ungraded homework were compared. No significant difference in conceptual understanding of the material was seen between sections, despite students with graded homework reporting more time spent studying outside of class.

Bonham, S., R. Beichner and D. Deardorff (2001). "Online Homework: Does It Make a Difference?" *Physics Teacher* **39**(5): 293-296. DOI: 10.1119/1.1375468

The authors examined the effect of online homework compared with written homework in introductory physics courses. Back-to-back sections were taught by the same teacher with the same content, but varied homework format. Exam grades for the sections were not significantly different. Web-based homework was well received, even though students with web-based homework reported spending more time on homework. In spite of there being no apparent benefit to student performance, web-based homework has several advantages. Teaching assistants are not needed for grading, freeing them for other aspects of the course. In classes where homework is not given or not graded, web-based homework might afford significant benefits.

Collard, D. M., S. P. Girardot and H. M. Deutsch (2002). "From the Textbook to the Lecture: Improving Prelecture Preparation in Organic Chemistry." *Journal of Chemical Education* **79**(4): 520-523. DOI: 10.1021/ed079p520

A technique for encouraging students to read the textbook and study the material before class is described. This method is complementary to traditional lecturing methods, providing a way to use new teaching pedagogies to make the lectures more meaningful and productive. Prelecture assignments, called HWebs, are given on textbook reading assignments relevant to the next class lecture; these assignments are composed of three multiple-choice questions ranging from simple recognition problems to more complex synthesis problems. Assignments are submitted and graded online, and answers are discussed in the next class period. Students reported often reading the textbook before coming to class and that this use of the textbook increased their understanding of the material. Though no correlation was found between grade and attitude regarding the assignments, students who did better on the assignments did better in other areas of the course.

Day, J. A. and J. D. Foley (2006). "Evaluating a Web Lecture Intervention in a Human-Computer Interaction Course." *IEEE Transactions on Education* **49**(4): 420-431. DOI: 10.1109/TE.2006.879792

This paper describes the use of web lectures viewed prior to class as a means of freeing up class time for active learning activities. Lectures were prepared using widely available software, and were kept to 15 to 25 minutes while covering approximately the same amount of material as a typical 30 to 50 minute classroom lecture. Lecture homework assignments (LHWs) were used to motivate students to view the web lecture in advance of class time. To test the format, two sections of a course were compared, one using the web lectures and frequent in-class activities, the other in a traditional lecture format. Several controls were implemented, including decreasing the class meeting for the experimental section to account for the out-of-class time students spent viewing the web lectures. Results showed that students in the experimental section scored better, though not statistically significantly, in all aspects of the course, and received overall higher grades (statistically significant). Additionally, student attitudes were assessed four times throughout the semester, revealing that students viewed the web lectures and the experimental course format positively. Both sections viewed the LHWs as helpful in focusing studying and learning the material.

Dobson, J. L. (2008). "The use of formative online quizzes to enhance class preparation and scores on summative exams." *Advances in Physiology Education* **32**(4): 297-302. DOI: 10.1152/avan.90162.2008

The author examines the use of formative online quizzes in an undergraduate exercise physiology course. Approximately weekly online quizzes were given to encourage students to complete and critically think about the reading for the class meetings. Quizzes were made available for 48 hours, typically the 48 hours before the first class meeting of the week. Students were allowed exactly 15 minutes to complete each quiz. Since the quizzes are meant to be a tool of formative assessment, they were worth 1% of the course grade, a small percentage meant to encourage students to participate and take it seriously, but without being threatening or stressful. Compared with previous sections of the course, where no online quizzes were given, students given online quizzes performed significantly better.

Klionsky, D. J. (2001). "Constructing Knowledge in the Lecture Hall." *Journal of College Science Teaching* **31**(4): 246-251. *http://www.nsta.org/store/product_detail.aspx?id=10.2505/4/jcst01_031_04_246*

The author describes a strategy to encourage students to read and study consistently outside of class. Lecture notes are given in advance of the class in lieu of textbook reading assignments. These notes include an outline as well as "guideline questions," which are questions on key concepts from the reading that students should be able to answer. Additionally, some lecture time was replaced with problem solving sessions. No exams or finals were given; instead, students were graded on daily reading and concept quizzes only. This approach has many advantages, such as increased participation and frequent feedback. Weaknesses are also addressed, such as the amount of time necessary to implement the strategy. The author also makes a comparison to lecture-only courses and found that students rated the course higher when this strategy was used. Students also performed better than in a lecture-only version of the course.

Moravec, M., A. Williams, N. Aguilar-Roca and D. K. O'Dowd (2010). "Learn before Lecture: A Strategy That Improves Learning Outcomes in a Large Introductory Biology Class." *CBE-Life Sciences Education* **9**(4): 473-481. DOI: 10.1187/cbe.10-04-0063

The authors examined the effect of introducing new material before class with required pre-class assignments. Three types of learn before lecture (LBL) assignments were examined: a narrated PowerPoint video with required note-taking, a one-page worksheet based on textbook reading, and a hands-on cut-out project (construction of a plasmid DNA molecule). Final exam questions specifically addressing the material covered by these assignments were compared over three years with LBLs introduced in the third year. Two sections in the third year were compared to examine the effect of the different LBL methods. Results show that students in the LBL year scored higher on multiple-choice questions than in the previous years, though no difference was observed in the short answer questions. The three LBL methods examined were shown to be equally effective. Student attitudes towards the LBLs were overall positive. The LBL method is shown to be an effective way to increase student understanding of topics. Since the LBLs can be introduced for just one or two topics at a time, instructors can gradually modify their classes.

Inquiry-Based Learning Techniques
Bailey, C. P., V. Minderhout and J. Loertscher (2012). "Learning transferable skills in large lecture halls: Implementing a POGIL approach in biochemistry." *Biochemistry and Molecular Biology Education* **40**(1): 1-7. DOI: 10.1002/bmb.20556

A case study in implementing POGIL (process oriented, guided-inquiry learning), this paper describes active learning activities in a large biochemistry class. The class of ~180 students met in a large lecture hall with fixed seating, so student groups were formed of three or four, the largest number that could easily communicate with each other. Each 75-minute class began with a 10-15 minute mini-lecture followed by a POGIL activity. After the activity, the remaining time is used for a second mini-lecture or POGIL activity, clicker questions, or think-pair-share, depending on how the class responds to the initial activity. The authors also describe the analogy to practicing sports used to get students to "buy-in" to this new way of learning. Students made significant conceptual gains with the new class (Villafañe, Bailey, Loertscher, Minderhout and Lewis 2011).

Barrows, H. S. (1996). "Problem-based learning in medicine and beyond: A brief overview." *New Directions for Teaching and Learning* **1996**(68): 3-12. DOI:10.1662/0002-7685(2003)065[0491:asattg]2.0.co;2

This paper presents a brief history of the development of problem-based learning in medical schools, and a thorough definition of the method is given. The main educational objectives of the method are discussed, as are issues of adopting problem-based learning and developing curricula. Though the paper focuses on medical education, it serves as a good introduction to important aspects of problem-based learning.

Blair, A. C., E. R. Fisher and D. Rickey (2012). "Discovering Nanoscience." *Science* **337**(6098): 1056-1057. DOI: 10.1126/science.1215151

This essay describes Model-Observe-Reflect-Explain (MORE) Thinking Frame, an inquiry-based instructional approach which has been shown to increase students' understanding of science. Using the MORE Thinking Frame, the students describe their ideas about a particular system, conduct experiments about the system, then return to their original ideas to refine them, completing an iteration of MORE.

Chaplin, S. (2009). "Assessment of the Impact of Case Studies on Student Learning Gains in an Introductory Biology Course." *Journal of College Science Teaching* 39(1): 72-79. *http://www.nsta.org/store/product_detail.aspx?id=10.2505/4/jcst09_039_01_72*

The author describes the use of case studies in an introductory biology course. Portions of lectures were replaced with several days of examining a case study. Students are briefly introduced to the topic, and then work individually on part of the case study using the textbook as a reference. In the following class period, the class discusses questions posed in the case study and new information from the textbook. Two sections in non-sequential years are compared, one taught using only traditional lecturing, the second using case studies. In the case study section, more students showed improvement over the course of the term. Additionally, students in the case study section were more able to apply their knowledge in application-analysis-type questions, indicating an increase in higher-order thinking skills.

Coppola, B. (1996). "Progress in Practice: Teaching and Learning with Case Studies." *Chemical Educator* **1**(4): 1. DOI: 10.1007/s00897960050a

This paper provides a good description of the details of using case studies in instruction. Included are characteristics of good cases, a detailed example of implementation, and several examples of cases.

Fukami, T. (2013). "Integrating Inquiry-Based Teaching with Faculty Research."
Science **339**(6127): 1536-1537. DOI: 10.1126/science.1229850

This essay from a Science Prize for Inquiry-Based Instruction (IBI) winner
briefly describes development and format of an inquiry-based biology course
at Stanford University.

Hein, S. M. (2012). "Positive Impacts Using POGIL in Organic Chemistry."
Journal of Chemical Education **89**(7): 860-864. DOI: 10.1021/ed100217v

This paper discusses the use of process-oriented, guided-inquiry learning
(POGIL) in a year-long organic chemistry sequence. Students were monitored
over six years, three taught using traditional lectures, three using the POGIL
method. After the second semester, a standardized exam was administered
as the final exam. Scores on this exam were compared for the six years
to evaluate the effect of POGIL on student assessments. There was no
significant difference in the average national percentile rankings between
the traditional sections and the POGIL sections when using the same form of
the standardized exam (a new form was implemented part-way through the
study). A significant decrease was observed in the number of students scoring
in the 25th percentile or below upon implementation of the POGIL method.
This suggests that the POGIL method does have a positive impact on student
learning, having the greatest effect on lower-achieving students.

Jackson, D. P., P. W. Laws and S. V. Franklin (2012). "An Inquiry-Based
Curriculum for Nonmajors." *Science* **335**(6067): 418-419. DOI: 10.1126/
science.1213444

This essay describes the Explorations in Physics (EiP) curriculum, which uses
inquiry to increase scientific literacy of non-science majors. The curriculum
emphasizes student-driven inquiry as a way of understanding the reality of
ambiguities, measurement errors, and other uncertainties in science.

Yadav, A., M. Lundeberg, M. DeSchryver, K. Dirkin, N. A. Schiller, K. Maier and
C. F. Herreid (2007). "Teaching Science with Case Studies: A National Survey of
Faculty Perceptions of the Benefits and Challenges of Using Cases."
Journal of College Science Teaching **37**(1): 34-38. ISSN-0047-231X

This article presents the results of a survey of faculty using case studies in
their courses and addresses the perceived benefits and obstacles. Generally,
faculty view using case studies in instruction as beneficial, with few obstacles.

Just-in-Time Teaching

Marrs, K. A. and G. Novak (2004). "Just-in-Time Teaching in Biology: Creating an Active Learner Classroom Using the Internet." *Cell Biology Education* **3**(1): 49-61. DOI: 10.1187/cbe.03-11-0022

The authors provide a summary of Just-in-Time Teaching (JiTT), and describe how it has been adopted by two different courses. JiTT combines active learning constructivism and formative assessment to more fully engage both student and instructor, and relies on web-based course content to create a feedback loop between student and instructor. Three key aspects of JiTT are discussed in the paper: warm-up assignments, interactive lectures, and "What is Biology Good For" extra credit assignments. Weekly warm-up exercises are designed to identify student misconceptions and prior knowledge. This information is then used during class to address the misconceptions directly. Lectures described here consist of a short lecture/discussion for the first third of the class time, followed by cooperative learning exercises tied to the warm-up exercises. "What is Biology Good For" are extra credit assignments that address biology in the news or address topics not covered in the course, and help students connect their classroom activities with the outside world. JiTT has several benefits: increasing classroom interactivity, providing ongoing formative assessment, and increasing retention rates, class preparation, and study habits. The authors note that while JiTT does require a large time commitment from instructors to implement, small portions of the program can be implemented at a smaller time cost and still be effective.

Novak, G., A. Gavrin and E. Patterson (2004). "Just-In-Time teaching." *http://jittdl.physics.iupui.edu/jitt/*

This website introduces the Just-In-Time teaching (JiTT) method, including resources and contact information of instructors/professors using JiTT.

Student Self-Assessment and Concept Inventories

Bauer, C. F. (2005). "Beyond "Student Attitudes": Chemistry Self-Concept Inventory for Assessment of the Affective Component of Student Learning." *Journal of Chemical Education* **82**(12): 1864-1870. DOI: 10.1021/ed082p1864

This paper describes the development and initial uses of an instrument, the chemistry self-concept inventory or CSCI, for measuring student attitudes in and towards chemistry. The CSCI seeks to better define "attitude" by differentiating several different mental constructs underlying the term, such as beliefs, interests, and understanding of the nature of science. The instrument is based on the well-developed Self-Description Questionnaire III (SDQIII), which has been shown to be strongly valid and reliable; however, as the SDQIII does not address attitude towards science or chemistry, 10 of 40 questions were modified to address attitudes towards the subject of chemistry.

The remaining questions probe attitudes towards mathematics, academics, academic enjoyment, and creativity. In the CSCI instrument, students rank their agreement with statements on a 7-point scale from "very accurate of me" to "very inaccurate of me." The instrument was tested on diverse student populations, establishing validity and reliability. The CSCI instrument is useful in understanding how students perceive themselves in chemistry, mathematics, academic performance, academic enjoyment, and creativity. While the absolute scores are not necessarily meaningful, pre- and post-tests will provide significant insight into how students respond to a course or new teaching approaches.

Bauer, C. F. (2008). "Attitude toward Chemistry: A Semantic Differential Instrument for Assessing Curriculum Impacts." *Journal of Chemical Education* **85**(10): 1440-1445. DOI: 10.1021/ed085p1440

This paper describes a survey instrument for assessing student attitudes towards chemistry and describes an initial use with a group of students. The ASCI, or Attitude towards the Subject of Chemistry Inventory, has respondents describe their attitude towards chemistry by choosing on a 7-point scale between two polar adjectives, such as exciting or boring. Adjectives were chosen that are conversationally relevant and understandable to college-age respondents. Adjectives could be grouped into several categories, allowing for averaging in these categories; categories included interest and utility, anxiety, intellectual accessibility, fear, and emotional satisfaction. The survey was given to students in a general chemistry course in two different years, as well as to peer leaders, chemistry majors, and non-science majors. Analysis of attitudes revealed several predictable responses: non-science majors rated highest in anxiety and fear and students with little experience with chemistry rated low on interest and utility. The ASCI provides a means to measure students' emotions, and can be used before and after or throughout a course.

Denofrio, L. A., B. Russell, D. Lopatto and Y. Lu (2007). "Linking Student Interests to Science Curricula." *Science* **318**(5858): 1872-1873. DOI: 10.1126/science.1150788

This paper presents an example of the use of the Classroom Undergraduate Research Experience (CURE) survey. The survey was used to evaluate the "Chemistry and Biology of Everyday Life" course, where students are matched with courses and research groups based on their background and interests. The CURE survey was used to show that students benefited from the program by progressing in several areas important for scientific research.

Grove, N. and S. L. Bretz (2007). "CHEMX: An Instrument to Assess Students' Cognitive Expectations for Learning Chemistry." *Journal of Chemical Education* **84**(9): 1524-1529. DOI: 10.1021/ed084p1524

This paper describes the development and initial testing of an instrument, the Chemistry Expectations Survey or CHEMX, to assess student perceptions of what is expected of them for learning chemistry. These expectations affect the attitudes students have about chemistry and the decisions they make about such things as class attendance and time commitment to a class. Knowing these expectations can help faculty understand their students better and perhaps address differences in expectations between faculty and students. The CHEMX is based on the Maryland Physics Expectations Survey (MPEX) and contains statements from MPEX as well as a modified statement addressing chemistry more specifically. Respondents are asked to rank their agreement with each statement on a 5-point scale. The statements cover seven areas. Statements on effort probe the extent to which a student devotes time and energy to studying. Concept statements query if the student contemplates underlying concepts and ideas rather than simply memorizing facts and formulas. Math link statements probe whether the student considers math and chemistry as interrelated. Reality link statements examine if the student connects chemistry concepts and ideas with life outside the classroom. Outcome statements probe the extent to which the student values learning chemistry: as essential to career goals or as an obstacle. Laboratory statements examine whether the student understands the concepts being used in experiments or is only following the procedures. Visualization statements query the extent to which the student regards visualization of atoms or molecules as important. Survey data from undergraduates at four diverse institutions were gathered, allowing comparisons between expectations of faculty and students as well as across several student populations. Significant differences existed between faculty and beginning general chemistry students, while more advanced students showed expectations closer to those of the faculty.

Hake, R. R. (1998). "Interactive-engagement versus traditional methods: a six-thousand student survey of mechanics test data for introductory physics course." *American Journal of Physics* **66**(1): 64-74. DOI: 10.1119/1.18809

The paper describes a survey of a physics diagnostic test and concept inventory based on literature review and personal communication to determine the effectiveness of interactive engagement, defined as classroom activities that yield immediate feedback through discussion, compared with traditional instruction. A detailed statistical analysis of the results reveals that interactive engagement courses are much more effective than traditional courses at teaching students basic concepts. Limitations and sources of error in the study are also discussed in detail.

Kennepohl, D., M. Guay and V. Thomas (2010). "Using an Online, Self-Diagnostic Test for Introductory General Chemistry at an Open University." *Journal of Chemical Education* **87**(11): 1273-1277. DOI: 10.1021/ed900031p

Authors describe an online, self-diagnostic test for prediction of student success in general chemistry. The test analyzes student background, conceptual basics, critical thinking, mathematical skills, and problem solving. Rather than predicting grades, this optional test gives students information about their preparedness for the course, and allows students to proactively address problems by seeking remedial help or redirecting their studies. Authors found that performance on the critical thinking section of the test correlated well with student performance on examinations and assignments while the conceptual basics correlated with laboratory performance. Surprisingly, a very weak correlation was found between student background in chemistry and performance in the course.

Lopatto, D. "CURE Survey — Assessment Instruments." Retrieved August 1, 2013, from *http://www.grinnell.edu/academic/csla/assessment/cure*.

The website for the Classroom Undergraduate Research Experience (CURE) survey contains a brief introduction to the survey, which is designed to measure the experiences of students in research-centric courses. In addition to containing links for the pre- and post-test, the page lists several published uses of the CURE survey.

Lopatto, D. (2004). "Survey of Undergraduate Research Experiences (SURE): First Findings." *Cell Biology Education* **3**(4): 270-277. DOI: 10.1187/cbe.04-07-0045

This paper describes the use of the SURE instrument to measure the effect of undergraduate research on career plans. The survey queries demographic information, learning gains, and aspects of summer research programs. Students from 41 institutions have participated in the survey. Almost all students (91%) reported that their research experience sustained or increased their interest in continuing their science education. Additionally, students reported benefits in a number of areas related to science research, such as understanding of the research process, learning of lab techniques, and self-confidence.

McFate, C. and J. Olmsted (1999). "Assessing Student Preparation through Placement Tests." *Journal of Chemical Education* **76**(4): 562-565. DOI: 10.1021/ed076p562

This paper analyzes several common chemistry placement tests for their ability to predict student success in general chemistry, as defined by a grade of C or higher. It identifies abilities required for success in chemistry, rather than knowledge. The authors address effectiveness of placement tests at predicting success and the types of questions that are particularly effective predictors.

Seymour, E., D. J. Wiese, A.-B. Hunter and S. M. Daffinrud (2000). "Creating a Better Mousetrap: On-line Student Assessment of their Learning Gains." *National Meeting of the American Chemical Society Symposium*. San Francisco, CA. *http://www.salgsite.org/docs/SALGPaperPresentationAtACS.pdf*

The authors discuss development of a tool for assessing student learning gains as a more insightful alternative to standard course evaluations. Standard course evaluations are perceived by faculty to poorly judge the efficacy of their teaching, provide little useful feedback, and ask the "wrong" questions. However, these same evaluations are used by departments and administrators to judge teaching effectiveness for promotion or tenure. The tool described here attempts to guide students to give realistic feedback on and discuss how much they have gained in specific aspects of the course, rather than asking about liking or disliking such aspects as the teacher, the course, or the textbook. This targeted feedback allows faculty to specifically address areas that need improvement or change. A template (available free online) provides sample questions in sections related to different aspects of the course, such as lab activities, or skill development, such as writing. Students rate the helpfulness of aspects of the course on a scale of 1 (was of no help) to 5 (was of very much help). The authors also discuss how to word questions so as to evoke the most detailed and useful answers. Poor questions end up with students drawing upon traditional course standards (lecture format) for comparison or are unnecessarily polarizing (liking or not liking something). The most helpful responses were to questions such as "what was missing from the course," "what suggestions do you have for us in revising the class." The authors also describe testing with faculty at a variety of institutions, and discuss how these faculty members altered the template, how quickly students responded, and what student feedback they received about the tool.

Seymour, E., D. Wiese, A.-B. Hunter and S. M. Daffinrud.
"Student Assessment of Learning Gains." Retrieved November 5, 2012, from
http://www.wcer.wisc.edu/archive/cl1/oldflag/cat/salg/salg7.htm

This website provides a good overview of the SALG instrument. The site provides instructions for using the instrument, as well as tips, limitations, and a list of pros and cons of the instrument.

Villafañe, S. M., C. P. Bailey, J. Loertscher, V. Minderhout and J. E. Lewis (2011). "Development and analysis of an instrument to assess student understanding of foundational concepts before biochemistry coursework." *Biochemistry and Molecular Biology Education* **39**(2): 102-109. DOI: 10.1002/bmb.20464

The authors report on the development and validation of an instrument to measure eight concepts that are prerequisites for biochemistry. These concepts were drawn from general chemistry and biology courses and represent essential knowledge for understanding biochemistry. Three questions for each concept are included in the test, which can be used as both pre- and post-tests. The authors developed a useful instrument, which can be obtained by contacting them. Additionally, they clearly outlined their method for developing and validating the instrument, allowing others to more easily design instruments in the future.

Virtual Labs and Computer Simulations

de Jong, T., M. C. Linn and Z. C. Zacharia (2013). "Physical and Virtual Laboratories in Science and Engineering Education." *Science* **340**(6130): 305-308. DOI: 10.1126/science.1230579

This review paper summarizes the current literature comparing virtual and physical laboratories. Virtual experiments have certain advantages, such as less set-up time and the ability of students to perform multiple trials. Additionally, equipment malfunctions are less likely to cause problems in virtual experiments. The authors cite several studies showing no difference in conceptual understanding by students performing physical or virtual labs. The authors also describe several studies effectively combining virtual and physical labs.

Yaron, D., M. Karabinos, D. Lange, J. G. Greeno and G. Leinhardt (2010). "The ChemCollective — Virtual Labs for Introductory Chemistry Courses." *Science* **328**(5978): 584-585. DOI: 10.1126/science.1182435

This essay describes an online digital library, the ChemCollective (www.chemcollective.org), which includes a virtual lab to increase students' conceptual understanding of chemistry ideas. This resource is intended to supplement textbook problem-solving, not replace physical laboratory experience. Within the virtual lab, students can design and perform experiments that may not be possible in a physical lab. Additionally, some activities use real-world examples. The authors briefly describe the results of a study (Leinhardt, Cuadros and Yaron 2007) *Journal of Chemical Education,* showing that the virtual lab contributed significantly to learning.

Writing in Response to Lecture

Butler, A., K.-B. Phillmann and L. Smart (2001). "Active Learning within a Lecture: Assessing the Impact of Short, In-Class Writing Exercises." *Teaching of Psychology* **28**(4): 257-259. DOI: 10.1207/s15328023top2804_04

The authors describe an exercise that is a combination of minute papers and think-pair-share. In this exercise, students are prompted with a question related to the lecture topic. Students answer the question on index cards, then exchange cards and discuss the answers in groups of two or three. Several final exam questions were linked with questions from the exercise; students' performance on these questions was compared between a section that used the exercise and one that did not. For one-third of these final exam questions (4 of 12), performance of students who used the exercise was better than those who did not. Of the remaining questions, performance was the same for seven, and worse for one. While this is only a small success, the exercise is quick and easy to implement.

Harwood, W. S. (1996). "The One-Minute Paper: A Communication Tool for Large Lecture Classes." *Journal of Chemical Education* **73**(3): 229-230. DOI: 10.1021/ed073p229

The "one-minute paper" is described as a tool to increase communication between the instructor and a large lecture class. The lecture is ended early, and students are given an opportunity to anonymously write down one main point from the lecture and one question they have. In the following class, some questions may be praised (to encourage good questions) and addressed. Students quickly become more confident at asking questions, and more students ask questions during lecture. Also, the instructor can quickly address confusion and misconceptions. Additionally, the students praise and criticize the instructor, providing positive feedback and opportunity for improvement.

Paulson, D. R. (1999). "Active Learning and Cooperative Learning in the Organic Chemistry Lecture Class." *Journal of Chemical Education* **76**(8): 1136-1140. DOI: 10.1021/ed076p1136

See Cooperative Learning *section*

Strauss, M. and T. Fulwiler (1990). "Writing to Learn in Large Lecture Classes." *Journal of College Science Teaching* **19**(3): 158-63.

The author describes several ways to incorporate informal writing in a large lecture course. Students are instructed to write questions throughout the lecture period, which are submitted anonymously; selected questions are incorporated into the following lecture. Students are also encouraged to keep notebooks or logs of their thoughts and concerns as they study. Finally, group writing activities in laboratories are described.

References

Cheetham, R. D., L. Goodwin and J. E. Miller (1991). "Teaching freshmen to think — does active learning work?" *BioScience* **41**(10): 719-722.

Cheetham, R. D. and J. E. Miller (1990). "Teaching freshmen to think–active learning in introductory biology." *BioScience* **40**(5): 388-391.

Leinhardt, G., J. Cuadros and D. Yaron (2007). ""One Firm Spot": The Role of Homework as Lever in Acquiring Conceptual and Performance Competence in College Chemistry." *Journal of Chemical Education* **84**(6): 1047-1052. DOI: 10.1021/ed084 p1047

Miller, J. E., J. Wilkes, R. D. Cheetham and L. Goodwin (1993). "Tradeoffs in Student Satisfaction: Is the "Perfect" Course an Illusion?" *Journal on Excellence in College Teaching* **4**: 27-47.

Villafañe, S. M., C. P. Bailey, J. Loertscher, V. Minderhout and J. E. Lewis (2011). "Development and analysis of an instrument to assess student understanding of foundational concepts before biochemistry coursework." *Biochemistry and Molecular Biology Education* **39**(2): 102-109.